AMERICAN FASHION DESIGNERS AT HOME

COUNCIL OF FASHION DESIGNERS OF AMERICA

AMERICAN FASHION DESIGNERS AT HOME

COUNCIL OF FASHION DESIGNERS OF AMERICA

WRITTEN BY RIMA SUQI

FOREWORD BY MARGARET RUSSELL

ASSOULINE

CONTENTS

FOREWORD BY MARGARET RUSSELL

Editor in Chief, *Elle Decor*

Fashion design and fashionable decorating go hand in hand; we love watching colors, patterns, and themes from the runway glide into decor and vice versa. And, in fact, some of the most intriguing interiors of our time have been crafted by the same talents who reinvent themselves at least twice a year, as they conjure mystery and magic in their collections. This symbiotic relationship between fashion and the home never fails to inspire. Personal style is the aesthetic thread that leads from our closets into our daily lives, and at *Elle Decor,* we gravitate toward the trendsetters who create what we shop for and guide how we dress. Their homes offer unique insight into their points of view, presenting in a remarkably intimate manner how those who design for others choose to design for themselves.

When the Council of Fashion Designers of America invited its members to participate in this book project, the response was extraordinary. Everyone from neophyte stylists to fashion icons signed on. The result is a fascinating compilation of interiors, ranging from razzle-dazzle glamorous to quietly humble, in locales from Ramatuelle, France; to San Miguel de Allende, Mexico; to the verdant hills of Connecticut. These rooms are smart, stylish backgrounds to hectic lives, and the eclectic photographs document where and how these compelling personalities—all with demanding careers and high-profile lives—kick back and what life is like behind the fever and flash of the runway.

Many of the featured homes were familiar to me, having previously appeared in the pages of *Elle Decor* or other magazines, though some were a lovely surprise. All are deeply inspiring, because they showcase the originality, the passion, and the flair of the people who live in them. These are timeless interiors, rooms with conviction and confidence, the epitome of design that rings true.

Not long after *Elle Decor* featured Ricky and Ralph Lauren's family compound at the tip of Long Island, a friend told me that he respected the designer even more after seeing photographs of his home in the magazine. "The place isn't the least bit showy or ostentatious," he said. "You get the feeling they really have fun there. It's funny, but his clothing seems more authentic now that I know how Ralph Lauren really lives."

And that's the point of this remarkable book: The interiors reflect not only the magic these designers create on the runway but also the glamorous reality of modern fashionable lives well lived.

Opposite Designer Cynthia Rowley's dining room featuring wall covering she designed.

INTRODUCTION BY RIMA SUQI

"There's no question that I find houses and decorating absolutely fascinating. That really turns me on. That's when I get excited."

—Bill Blass

The words above may have been expressed by Bill Blass but they also reflect the sensibilities of many of the designers featured in this sixth offering in Assouline and the Council of Fashion Designers of America's American Fashion series. *American Fashion Designers at Home* presents the rare opportunity to visit, via gorgeous photographs, the residences of more than one hundred CFDA members. Previously published titles in the series provide insight into the evolution of fashion in our country and celebrate the work and significant contributions of our most legendary designers. On the pages of this book, we're ushered along on an intimate tour of the designers' ingenuity at home. The result is a visually fascinating and ultravoyeuristic peek into the way they live, the furnishings they choose, the artwork they collect, and the palettes they play with in their personal spaces.

Our homes are, after all, the ultimate reflections of our identities and aesthetic tastes. Each of the living quarters featured in this book offers insight into a designer's style on a very personal level. In some cases, the homes mirror the aesthetics of the designers' collections. Here we can experience Betsey Johnson's and Gene Meyer's use of color, Francisco Costa's luxurious minimalism, Cynthia Rowley's playful elegance, and Ralph Lauren's classic American style. But there are also charming surprises. Gary Wolkowitz, the owner of the colorful legwear company Hot Sox, lives in a Michael Gabellini–designed minimalist apartment, with stark white walls and a highly prized art collection. Isaac Manevitz, of

Opposite The library in Francisco Costa's Murray Hill apartment.

Ben-Amun jewelry, has amassed museum-quality pieces of Memphis collective furniture in his suburban New Jersey house. Lela Rose lives in a loft designed by alumni of Rem Koolhaas's Office for Metropolitan Architecture that is decidedly lacking in the feminine frills which characterize her fashions. Stephen Dweck's New Jersey beach house has the formality of a Park Avenue penthouse. Every turn of the page brings another revelation or unexpected tableau. There's not a dull moment—an ideal runway show, as it were.

Inspiration feeds creativity, and our surroundings can provide a platform for new ideas and influence our work, which might explain why some of the designers have multiple dwellings: A country barn, an island aerie, a mountain lodge, or a Parisian pied-à-terre can complement (and, in some cases, provide a substitute for) an urban lifestyle. It's another space to decorate, another impetus to get up early and scour the flea markets and estate sales, to forage for antiques in foreign lands, and to acquire art. It's a place to display an overflow of collections or items amassed in a storage space. And it can even be the catalyst for the launch of a home collection.

Home furnishing is a natural crossover for fashion designers, and one of the first to experiment with design outside his atelier was the couturier Charles James. He moved to the United States in the twenties, and after developing a name for sculpting ball gowns and intricate dresses that came to be respected as art, he went on to design interiors and create furniture for the renowned art patrons John and Dominique de Menil in their Houston home.

In the seventies, Halston extended his sexy beige aesthetic to his legendary Olympic Tower apartment and that of his good friend Liza Minnelli. He also designed the interiors and public spaces for Braniff International Airways. Bill Blass was a passionate collector but insisted on having a decorator guide him through the process of furnishing his home (luckily, he was friends with the likes of Mica Ertegun and Chessy Rayner). However, through his licensees (which at one point numbered more than fifty), he paved the way for fashion designers to expand into other categories. His name appeared on furniture, bed linens, towels, even backgammon sets, but he apparently drew the line at kitchen appliances. His success meant that the field was wide open for others—most notably Ralph

Lauren, Calvin Klein, the current CFDA president Diane von Furstenberg (whose home collection will debut next year), and many of the designers whose homes are featured in this book, including Oscar de la Renta, Donna Karan, Gene Meyer, Wenlan Chia, Nicole Miller, Tracy Reese, and Cynthia Rowley.

While fashion designers draw mostly on their own ideas when it comes to creating ready-to-wear, many will readily reference—and collect pieces from the estates of—other designers in their homes. Pauline Trigère, Halston, Oscar de la Renta, Carolina Herrera, Geoffrey Beene, and Bill Blass are some of the American legends who have influenced the personalities in this book. The sofa in Tory Burch's living room was inspired by one in Hubert de Givenchy's Paris home, and Ralph Rucci owns a pair of bronzes that once belonged to the French designer. Johan Lindeberg takes pride in pointing out that his dining table, bought at a flea market, once belonged to Norma Kamali. Francisco Costa has a screen previously owned by Horst—it's covered in fabric given to the photographer by none other than Coco Chanel. Another screen, from Geoffrey Beene's estate, now lives in Johnson Hartig's Los Angeles home, and a chair from Hattie Carnegie's legendary New York salon occupies a place of honor in Victor Costa's living room. The big winner in this category is Ron Chereskin, whose Fire Island beach house was owned by Halston. Oh, if those walls could talk.

Possessions (and homes) with a past have a staying power that few fashion items could ever achieve. Fashion is fun, but it can be fleeting and in a constant state of flux. Many of the designers interviewed admitted that while their offices and ateliers might reflect that energy, they prefer their homes to be more sedate and calming—a place of refuge to retreat to after a day (or a week) of hard work. While it's true that a house's main purpose is to provide shelter, a home is a different story—it represents values, commitment, and permanence. A home provides constancy, stability, and comfort, not for just a season or two, but for decades and, in many cases, for generations to come.

REEM ACRA

"No, I do not overstuff," says Reem Acra of her minimalist decorating philosophy. It's not that she doesn't have the room. The Lebanese-born designer, who made her name creating ultraluxurious bridal gowns, put two lofts together to form a thirty-two-hundred-square-foot apartment in New York City. "I loved the grandeur of the space when I walked in," she recalls. "It's big—it's got high ceilings and that open loft feeling." And now it has very blue walls. Why blue? "They're meant to match a 1920s fabric I bought at a flea market and used to upholster a settee." Indeed, many of her furnishings came from frequent excursions to flea markets, which she loves for reasons that go beyond the art of the deal. "You find things nobody would look at. You can transform them, and they can become the center of attention," she explains. "It's a good way to use your imagination and exercise your creativity."

Top left Acra collects "anything that has great color or texture" and is especially fond of little dolls. *Bottom left* Antique fabric on the settee inspired the blue wall color throughout the loft. The chandelier is a flea market find made of wrought iron with red glass hurricanes. A painting of a woman in a wedding dress was bought at auction; an inlaid mirror from Turkey hangs in the hallway. *Opposite* It looks antique, but Acra bought her bed after seeing a 1-inch-square photo in a catalog, and she's had it for 25 years. Embroidered curtains are draped like a canopy overhead, and an old military chest sits at the foot of the bed. *Previous pages* Acra's first ad campaign was shot by Ruven Afanador in 1999. "I couldn't stop looking at it and decided to blow it up and live with it. I had it made into wallpaper," she says. The sofa is a 1950s flea market piece she had reupholstered in fuchsia fabric.

MAX AZRIA

BCBG stands for "Bon Chic, Bon Genre" or "Good Style, Good Attitude," and judging from Max and Lubov Azria's home, the saying applies to their life as well as their brand. Their sixty-room colonial-style mansion dates to 1924 and was designed by architect Paul Williams, who was a celebrity favorite at that time (he created homes for Frank Sinatra and Lucille Ball, and designed the Beverly Hills Hotel). It once belonged to the writer Sidney Sheldon, the creator of *I Dream of Jeannie*. Located in Holmby Hills in Los Angeles and set on three acres, the property boasts a greenhouse with organically grown fruits and vegetables and four gardens in various styles: English, French, Japanese, and Moroccan. There's also a six-thousand-square-foot movie theater, a glass-enclosed tennis court, and a pool inlaid with 14-karat gold. And that's just the outside. The overall structure of the main house remained intact but interiors were completely redone and designed by Lubov, the creative director of BCBG, with the interior designer Aly Daly. Max was born in Tunisia; Lubov is from Ukraine. The decor reflects both their origins and their love of modern design.

Above The designer and his wife, Lubov. *Opposite* The living room features a custom-designed sofa with throw pillows by Jonathan Adler. Lubov's collection of starburst mirrors—some new, some antique— add sparkle to the wall. *Following pages left* A vintage chandelier is suspended from the 14-karat-gold-leafed ceiling in Max's office. Gaetano Pesce's whimsical Up 2000 series chair and ottoman for B&B Italia sit on a rug designed by Paul Smith for The Rug Company. *Following pages right* The pool house has a sitting room that doubles as a bedroom. Pieces such as the light fixtures and poufs are a nod to Max's North African heritage.

JEFFREY BANKS

"The morning the prospectus came out, I handed them my check and said, 'I'd like apartment 4B,'" recalls Jeffrey Banks of how he acquired his home of twenty-nine years. He spent a year looking before friends who worked across the street from the lower Fifth Avenue building that housed the After Six tuxedo company informed him it was being converted into a co-op. "I bribed the workmen and went over at lunch every day for a week, so I got to see every single apartment before anybody else." He got what he wanted and, for over a year, lived in the two bedroom with eighteen-and-a-half-foot ceilings with only a bed, a Parsons table, and a few chairs. "I had to wait a year before I had the money to do what I wanted with the space," he explains. Banks hired his friends Charles Swerz and Jerry Van Deelen to redesign, changing the two-bedroom with closets entirely too small for a clotheshorse into a one-bedroom with an office and a walk-in closet. It also involved eighteen coats of white lacquer, pine pocket doors, white canvas sofas, and custom-designed moldings throughout. The color-free apartment provides a perfect backdrop for the designer's growing collection of black-and-white fashion photography. And the neighborhood, once considered sketchy at best, has blossomed as well.

Top left Banks's designer, Charles Swerz, insisted on the John Dickinson chairs around the dining table. Although apprehensive at first, Banks now says they're one of his favorite things. *Bottom left* An antique rocking horse, purchased at Macy's, occupies a place of honor in the living room. *Opposite* One of the only bits of color in the apartment is the vintage Americana quilt on Banks's bed. A portrait of Fred Astaire is perched above the banquette.

DENNIS BASSO

Nancy Corzine is the type of interior designer who takes only one client a year, with the caveat that he or she must let her do whatever she wants. It's a condition that most fashion designers—and especially a grand one like Dennis Basso—would not agree to. But he relinquished control to his good friend and ended up with a house he calls absolutely fabulous. Basso and his partner, Michael Cominotto, use this house in the Hamptons (and their others in West Palm Beach and New York City) to entertain like crazy. The interiors were designed around the colors blue and white and are styled in the breezy, elegant manner often associated with the South of France (like a chair and an ottoman designed by Corzine and upholstered in a Brunschwig & Fils fabric, or a collection of Delft porcelain). As beautiful as the home is inside, the action usually takes place outside in a massive poolside pavilion (*right*) designed by Kenneth Alpert as an outdoor living room. The centerpiece is a brick fireplace that presides over a conversation area with JANUS et Cie sofas upholstered in Sunbrella fabrics, Nancy Corzine leather ottomans, and a large glass coffee table by Lorin Marsh. At two thousand square feet, the space can easily hold a hundred people, seated, for one of Basso's famous summer luncheons.

JOHN BARTLETT

Yes, that's a bright pink rug in the New York City apartment of the menswear designer John Bartlett. "It's surprising, but totally works," he admits. "My partner, John Etsy, designed it." The custom piece delineates the dining area from the design studio (both on the first floor of the two-level West Village apartment) and provides the perfect stage for a vintage dining table surrounded by plastic chairs from Kartell. Most of the pieces in this room are vintage—the chest on the left, the lamps on the chest, the chandelier, and the floor lamp. But the groovy swivel chair is new—a Ricardo Fasanello design; Bartlett chose the colors of both the seat and the upholstery—as are the full-size photos by Ellen Carey hung behind it.

SULLY BONNELLY

When a fashion designer trained as an architect and a world-class curator specializing in twentieth-century Mexican art create a home together, the result is almost guaranteed to be as interesting as it is stylish. Sully Bonnelly and Robert Littman were pioneers in New York's Flatiron district, where they bought this loft more than two decades ago. Lured by both the space (thirty-five hundred square feet) and its condition (Bonnelly has described it as a "wreck"), the duo found the project they were looking for. When they needed advice, they had a Rolodex of friends to call on including the legendary Andrée Putman (she suggested a Jean-Michel Frank sofa and club chairs in the living room), but overall they were left to their own übersophisticated instincts. This means that pieces by Jenny Holzer, Donald Judd, and Richard Serra mingle with first-century Roman urns and vintage modern furniture by stars such as Frank Gehry, Piero Fornasetti and Jacques Adnet. Bonnelly had always said he wanted a place where visitors would walk in and say "Wow!" and it's obvious his wish came true.

Left One enters to an elevated "room" with a corrugated cardboard chair by Frank Gehry, a Noguchi Cyclone table, a floor lamp by Jacques Adnet, and a wishbone-shaped wooden sculpture that's actually an old fishing net.

MICHAEL SIMON

Michael Simon's Connecticut home was a horse stable when he bought it and "still had the stalls and a bunch of assorted animals living in it," says the knitwear designer of the place he calls home after decades of New York City loft living. The pool, clearly, was a new addition, designed to look like a real pond. It is nestled in a yard that, Simon says, has grown over the years to include an "eclectic assortment of different plants producing various colors throughout the four seasons. It also gives us a sanctuary to get lost in, to separate us from the outside world."

ANDREW FEZZA

Andrew and Marilyn Fezza bought their New England clapboard-style home in Weston, Connecticut, because it had "good bones," then gutted the place to make additional space and bring more light to the rear of the house. They added a moving octagonal tower (left) as a dining nook off their kitchen and, outdoors, a dining pergola (far left) and an open sunroom off the living room. The pool got a facelift, too, with stones replacing wood decking and gray slate added to the pool itself to complement the "natural pond" look.

STEFAN MILJANICH

"I love the Cape. A lot of it has inspired my designs. It's kind of a natural fit," says the designer and creative director of Gilded Age, who's been frequenting the area for two decades. Miljanich's wife, Patricia Kindregen, hails from Boston; they bought their classic Cape Cod–style home about eight years ago in an area close to the water but nestled in a woodlike cove of tall Cape pine trees. "It's very much a Vineyard house," says Miljanich of the structure, which looks old but was built in the 1980s. "We're trying to keep it in the spirit of the island by making sure it isn't perfectly manicured—this is very much a 19th-century type of place."

TORY BURCH

There are those who believe there is no greater luxury than residing in a hotel and living an Eloise-type existence, room service included. Tory Burch created that life when she, with her three sons, took up residence at New York's famed Pierre Hotel. The designer combined three apartments with Central Park views to form the now nine-thousand-square-foot space. She tapped interior designer Daniel Romualdez (he designed her stores), who sketched his ideas on a napkin during dinner one night. The plan was to evoke the building's Georgian-era roots but in a youthful and modern way and the result is a warm and welcoming space where there's never a "do not disturb" sign on the door.

Above The designer in her library. *Right* Burch's living room has hunter green walls, a sofa inspired by one in Givenchy's Paris home, and a sisal area rug from a town outside Saint Tropez.

Opposite The designer has an extensive collection of Chinese porcelain—two examples sit on the mantel of the living room's marble fireplace. *Above* An Imari bowl sits on a 19th-century Russian writing table in Burch's library. The room was inspired by a similar one in Oscar de la Renta's home.

KEVIN CARRIGAN

Kevin Carrigan, creative director for CK Calvin Klein, Calvin Klein Jeans, and Calvin Klein, readily admits that Bill Blass's Connecticut home inspired the decor of the country house he shares with his partner, Tim Furzer, an architect. Previously, the British natives spent weekends on Fire Island, but the commute (which involves a drive to a ferry, and island rules that don't allow cars for summer residents) got the best of them. They found this sweet 1920s Cape Cod cottage six years ago in Bellport, Long Island, once a sleepy fishing village in an area that now attracts fashionistas galore. Carrigan was in charge of furnishings, while Furzer handled redistribution of the space. The result is a very elegant take on country with just the right mix of distressed and polished, structured and slouchy and, for a touch of whimsy, a taxidermied monkey.

Above Vintage Hans Wegner chairs gather around a contemporary table by e15. A modernist Murano glass chandelier hangs above it. *Opposite* The couple's bedroom opens onto the pool, and meals are often taken alfresco around a vintage table set with dinnerware and accessories from Calvin Klein Home.

JULIE CHAIKEN

For years Julie Chaiken lived a bicoastal life. Then she closed up shop in New York City and relocated her business to her hometown of San Francisco (she's from the East Bay). Who could blame her? The four-level Russian Hill home where she lives with her two kids and her husband, Scott Grigsby, has breathtaking views of the San Francisco Bay, the Golden Gate Bridge, and Alcatraz. The couple bought the midcentury modern home nine years ago and hired Orlando Diaz-Azcuy Design Associates to help with remodeling. It's a very serene space now, with a relatively neutral palette accented with subdued shades of blue, a hue that mimics the color of the bay outside. "The house had a great feeling the minute I walked in," remembers Chaiken. "But the view sold it."

Above The designer in her bedroom with her son, Ethan. David Hockney's *Tulips* hangs above. *Top right* From the Novasuede-walled master bedroom, Chaiken has views north to Alcatraz Island. The crystal bedside lamps are from the 1930s and attributed to Samuel Marx. *Bottom right* As many as ten people can sit on Christian Liaigre chairs at Chaiken's vintage Robsjohn-Gibbings dining table. The area rug and cantilevered limestone shelf were designed by Greg Stewart; the painting above the shelf is *Sin-Without* by Ed Ruscha. *Opposite* Cy Twombly's *Roman Notes* hangs above a sofa designed by Greg Stewart. The coffee table is ebonized bamboo veneer from Wyeth with slipper chairs designed by Michael Taylor for Baker Furniture, circa 1952.

WENLAN CHIA

Wenlan Chia took advantage of post–September 11 real estate rental deals to move from a tiny one-bedroom above a Gap store in Midtown Manhattan to a fifteen-hundred-square-foot loftlike space in the financial district. It's significantly more room for the designer, her husband, Bernard Lin, and their French bulldog, Milan. "The walls and floors are white, and the kitchen is black. It's a nice backdrop to do what I want with the space—it doesn't take much to dress it up." And dress it up she did. Wenlan is very into pattern—she calls herself a Marimekko nut—and has a home collection of bedding, rugs, and throw pillows. Twinkle Living, as it's called, is a plethora of color and pattern, from geometric to traditional-with-a-twist. She mixed these pieces with vintage modern furniture, sourced both at home and abroad. While patterns liven up the loft, Chia kept the furnishings on the spare side: "I like a minimal style," she says. "I need to leave room for myself!"

Top left Chia *(above)* designed the rug underneath the Louis Ghost chairs by Philippe Starck and Tulip table by Eero Saarinen. The chandelier is Scandinavian and the credenza is vintage Knoll. *Bottom left* The bed is one of the only non-vintage pieces in the home; pillows from Twinkle Living home collection. The art above was bought at a charity auction. *Opposite* The building has communal roof access; Chia styled an outdoor sofa with her fabrics and throw pillows.

Right Chia shipped an original-edition Arco floor lamp (by Achille and Pier Giacomo Castiglioni) back from France; she found it at the Paris flea market. She recovered the Knoll sofas in navy cotton twill; she is hoping the swivel chairs are a Dunbar design. The coffee table is early George Nelson.

EVA CHOW

As a young design student, Eva Chow had the gumption to hire a limo to chauffeur her entire collection to what was undoubtedly one of the most fashionable stores in New York: Linda Dresner. Dresner bought it on the spot. Decades later Chow, who is married to the restaurateur Michael Chow of Mr. Chow fame, is no longer in the clothing business but does design her own jewelry as well as the restaurants in her husband's growing empire. Neither shies away from the spotlight and, at thirty thousand square feet, their Holmby Hills, Los Angeles, estate is impossible to ignore. From the limestone facade to the large antique carved doors at the entrance, everything here makes a statement. The main house, built from the ground up over a period of seven years (during which time the Chows lived in the Beverly Hills Hotel and a rented home in Bel Air), has five bedrooms, nine bathrooms, a library, a formal living room, family room, dining room, kitchen, wine cellar, swimming pool, and an underground garage. At five thousand square feet, the comparatively small one-bedroom guesthouse, with its gym, music room, and thirty-eight-seat, underground, state-of-the-art cinema, provides a view of swimmers in the pool from its acrylic windows. The Chows' visit to the Reina Sofia Museum, in Madrid, inspired the design of their home, and while Michael designed most of it himself (he also designed the Giorgio Armani boutique in Los Angeles), he did tap the Mexican architect Humberto Artigas to help with the Spanish structural elements. The resulting estate—which references both Spanish and Chinese architecture—houses the couple's large collection of portraits and museum-quality art deco furniture, and, of course, Eva's magnificent collection of couture.

Above The pool house has a waterproof indoor cinema; the pool itself is surrounded by rain fountains. *Opposite* Michael Chow is a huge fan of Emile-Jacques Ruhlmann's work; two desks designed by the Frenchman sit in the Macassar wood-paneled library, in front of a 16th-century Belgian tapestry depicting David's triumph over Goliath. Another desk is by Jean-Michel Frank. *Following pages left* Above the fireplace hangs a painting of Eva Chow in her Vivienne Westwood wedding gown, as visualized by Julian Schnabel. (At the opposite end of this room is another fireplace with a Basquiat portrait of Michael Chow hanging above.) *Following pages right* Real gold-leaf walls in the living room offset a sofa and armchairs by French architect Pierre Chareau; an 18th-century Murano glass chandelier hangs above.

DAVID CHU

David Chu considered a career in architecture or advertising before stumbling into fashion on the advice of a drawing instructor who took interest in his work. After founding Nautica (he sold the company seven years ago), he now helms David Chu Bespoke, offering custom suits for discerning gentlemen, and a sportswear line called LINCS by David Chu. Clearly change was in the air. Chu, his wife, Gina, and daughters, Bianca and Christie had been living in Greenwich, Connecticut, but chose to leave the preppy haven to return to the energy of the city. Chu, who was reluctant to leave the calm of Connecticut, called the move a "big change." But he was able to find a version of city calm high above Manhattan's often crazy streets, in a 1920s Park Avenue building that used to be a hotel. He bought the duplex as a raw space, and hired his younger brother Peter to oversee the renovation into a thirteen-room apartment suitable for a family. (Chu also owns a six-story town house that headquarters his custom business.) Surfaces were kept neutral— from dark-stained floors to linen-colored walls—as were furnishings (mostly Asian antiques from Chu's vast and growing collection) and art.

Opposite Chu designed several pieces of the furniture in his home, including desks in his study, a ceiling fixture in the dining room, and the sofas and side tables in his living room, featured here. *Following pages left* A painting by Dutch artist Jan Grotenbreg provides a moody backdrop for a wooden sculpture, originally from a temple in Thailand. *Following pages right* A Mongolian rug protects part of the limestone entryway; an antique Buddha stationed next to a lucky bamboo plant presides over the rest.

PETER LINDBERG

JACKIE ROGERS

"I knew I wanted to buy my house before I even went inside," says Jackie Rogers of her Wainscott, New York, home. The former model, who once worked for Coco Chanel and appeared in Fellini movies, loved the rustic charm of this cottage, made from wood salvaged from old Amish barns. She filled it with pieces she describes as "eclectic, both antique and new, with a strong Asian influence," like the red lacquer coffee table (a Japanese antique), lacquered Chinese Coromandel chairs and an antique bridal chest, also Chinese. The fur throw is new, but faux, lynx.

ISAAC MANEVITZ

Design aficionados should be salivating at this photo. In the relatively unassuming entrance to Isaac Manevitz's New Jersey home sit two very important pieces of furniture—an end table designed by Michele de Lucci in 1984 and a sofa designed by Peter Shire in 1986, both produced by Memphis, a furniture collective founded in the 1980s by Ettore Sottsass and others. Turns out that Manevitz, the designer of Ben-Amun jewelry, is a collector of Memphis furniture. His other pieces include the totemlike Carlton shelf and the Treetops lamp, both designed by Sottsass, and four chairs by de Lucci. This could well be the best-kept secret in fashion.

DAVID MEISTER

David Meister has built a reputation as the go-to guy for glamorous gowns seen on red carpets the world over. The modern Palm Springs, California, home the Los Angeles–based designer shares with his partner, Alan Siegel, is equally so: "We wanted [this] house to be glamorous and sexy," he explains. The custom Yamaha piano in white lacquer with silver plating, and the silk-screen portrait of Mick Jagger by British photographer–turned–music video director Russell Young both speak perfectly to that style.

PETER COHEN

"I am a closet architect," admits Peter Cohen. "It's the first visual language I truly understood, and it was something I was hugely interested in at another time in my life." Which explains the words the Zimbabwean native with his own eponymous fashion label uses to describe his 1957 Sherman Oaks home in Los Angeles's San Fernando Valley. "It is an intelligently designed house, perfectly placed on a hill to take advantage of the light and views, and designed by a good California modernist," he says of the three-bedroom, two-thousand-square-foot, L-shaped hideaway he bought six years ago. Even the garden was well designed—the house had been vacant for six months when Cohen bought it, yet the garden wasn't overgrown. "Because it's on a hilltop, it's more trees than shrubs," he explains. "It all takes care of itself."

Opposite A painting by Kenny Scharf decorates one side of the fireplace. Cohen made the cushions from sample fabric he had from Ratti, an Italian mill he often uses. The rug is an American hooked piece. *Above* Cohen says his pool is perfectly shaped because the design "predicts how you would walk around it. There are no surprises."

RACHEL COMEY

"This is my fantasy house," says Rachel Comey of the weekend home she purchased five years ago in Greenport, a small town on the North Fork of Long Island. The designer—who launched her collection as menswear only, but now focuses on women's wear and shoes for both sexes—grew up in Hartford, Connecticut, and wanted an escape that was nothing like the mountains and lakes of her youth. She craved a beach vibe and found it in this old fishing community, with the added bonus of a large, loftlike structure that's completely covered in vines. "It's an old industrial building that was a laundry in the 1920s," she says of her getaway. There had been several residents before Comey moved in, but when she took possession of the five-thousand-square-foot space she says she "didn't have to do much to it." It does have its quirks—half of the roof is made of the corrugated material used in greenhouses; the other half uses solar panels to pump energy back into the grid. But because the former allows filtered natural light to stream into the space from above and the latter makes it eco-friendly living, it's all good. As it should be.

Below The kitchen, with an island made of powder-coated steel and a butcher-block top, was left over from the previous residents. Comey says she loves to cook, and Greenport has many farm stands and fish markets that inspire her. *Opposite top* Comey in her fantasy home. *Opposite bottom* There's a large dining and living area with a long Pennsylvania farm table the designer bought on eBay. Half the Hans Wegner chairs around it are original; the other half are reproductions. The blue sofa is from a local shop called Beall & Bell.

FRANCISCO COSTA

Manhattan's Murray Hill is not traditionally a neighborhood that attracts a creative crowd. Yet it's where the Calvin Klein designer Francisco Costa and John DeStefano, his partner of more than a decade, chose to make their home. After living in a fancier neighborhood uptown, the duo bought their two-bedroom in a 1940s building about five years ago and hired the architecture firm PomaSteven to renovate the fourteen-hundred-square-foot space. It is minimal, but not starkly so, with the overall tone set by Costa's choice of color scheme— four shades of gray ranging from the very cool to the more saturated with purple undertones. Costa has said he finds the shades tranquil and complementary to the couple's art. Their collection is carefully edited and includes drawings by Jeff Koons in the entryway, photographs of Andy Warhol by Christopher Makos in the kitchen, a sculpture by Vik Muniz in the library, and a lithograph by Bruce Nauman. Most of the decor was chosen by the Brazilian-born designer, who met DeStefano while working at George Smith, a high-end British furniture boutique.

Opposite The screen in the living room once belonged to the photographer Horst and was made with fabric given to him by Coco Chanel. The horn chair, foreground, came from an early-19th-century Texas ranch. *Following pages left* A swing-out tractor seat under the window in the kitchen provides a perfect view of the Empire State Building. *Following pages right* A photograph of a horse's mane has a position of honor (DeStefano trains and manages horses).

GERHARD RICHTER

DUPRÉ - LAFON

OSCAR DE LA RENTA

Oscar de la Renta and his late wife, Françoise, bought their clapboard colonial home in Kent, Connecticut, in the early Seventies. De la Renta described the house he first saw as "nothing," but was immediately enchanted by the land around it. The designer, who once apprenticed with Cristóbal Balenciaga and was a couture assistant at Lanvin, is an avid gardener and had visions of what the site and the house could be. For some homeowners, bringing the outside in might involve adding windows and skylights, but for the de la Rentas it meant swathing their living and dining rooms in multiple layers of floral fabric (he once joked that there was so much fabric on the walls that the rooms had shrunk by at least an inch). Several years after Françoise passed away, de la Renta married his current wife, Annette. She had given up her country house for him, so de la Renta offered to build her a dream bedroom. She calls it her bedsit and, with the exception of a kitchen, it has all the necessities—a television, a desk area where Oscar can play his beloved computer solitaire, plenty of sofas for the dogs to sprawl out on, and a table where the couple can have dinner. It's a wonder they ever leave home.

Left Oscar and Annette de la Renta at the entrance to their Kent, Connecticut, home. *Above* The designer enlisted architect Ernesto Buch to create the bedsit, with living, dining, working, and sleeping areas. *Opposite top* It took three decades, but de la Renta created a series of garden rooms on his property; this one is the vegetable garden. *Opposite bottom* Annette's bathroom continues the tradition of upholstered walls in the home; the desk is an early Georgian antique. *Following pages* The Georgian-style bed, in what Annette calls her bedsit, is upholstered in a linen pattern called "Tree of Life," which the decorator Vivien Greenock procured at Robert Kime.

LOUIS DELL'OLIO

"This is a relaxing room," says Louis Dell'Olio of the porch in his Stamford, Connecticut, home. The designer, best known for his decades at Anne Klein and his wildly successful line for QVC, sourced furniture for the screened-in room from a place that supplies movie sets. He and his wife, Jacqueline, drove out to Pennsylvania, not knowing exactly what they'd find, and scored a beautiful set of old Bar Harbor wicker furniture, which is sturdier than the more ornate Victorian wicker. The cushions were custom made and, with that, the breezy room with views of the Long Island Sound was complete. "We sit here and watch boats sail by," says Dell'Olio. "It's just beautiful."

RANDOLPH DUKE

Randolph Duke says that the minute he saw the views from this Los Angeles property, he just "knew" it was home. Others knew too, and a bidding war ensued. But the born showman, who hails from Las Vegas, won. And with the three-lot spread came a small (fourteeen hundred square feet) home that clearly would not do. Enter Austin Kelly and Monika Häfelfinger of XTEN Architecture, who presented him with plans for what they called the Openhouse. And again, Duke knew. His three-bedroom home is spread over three levels and cantilevers out over the hillside and, thanks to the ten-foot-high retracting glass walls, the interior and exterior almost merge. Duke says the idea was to "get rid of walls" and, apparently, window treatments. There aren't any in the entire house, save for Duke's master suite, with its "curtains" of tiny metal beads. As Tobi Tobin, the designer Duke hired to decorate the house, so aptly put it: "The view is the jewelry of the house."

Below The so-called Openhouse designed by XTEN Architecture, has 270-degree views of Los Angeles. *Opposite* The former swimwear designer has two pools, lined with sparkling silver-leaf tiles. *Following pages* Duke had a hard time choosing the material for the two-story fireplace, and changed his mind "a hundred times" before settling on flat-cut, black-diamond granite. Duke and Tobin designed almost everything in the house that isn't antique, including the faux-fur throws on the custom-made sofas.

GILLES MENDEL

Gilles Mendel's apartment is as stylish as one would expect from a fifth-generation furrier who successfully steered the venerable company J. Mendel into the world of ready-to-wear. His bedroom is especially inviting, with a simple platform bed by Desiron set against a blood-red wall hung with a single graphic work by Max Gimblett. The bed is dressed with sheets from Frette and topped off with a luxurious chinchilla throw pillow and blanket that probably feels pretty wonderful against bare skin.

MICHAEL SPIRITO

"I put in my 'too cool for school years' in Williamsburg in the '90s,"
says Michael Spirito of his decision to move uptown to a duplex
apartment on New York City's Central Park West two years ago. This
corner of the upper level is where the jewelry designer (of the brand
Exhibitionist) likes to sketch—note the Venus flytrap set on his desk
for inspiration. Spirito made the chandelier himself: "I search for
antique bases, rewire them, and let myself go nuts with antique chairs,
crystals, porcelain tusks, and deer antlers." The mirror was a flea
market find he lacquered black, and a collection of carved amber
skulls sits on the windowsill, next to a tarantula box. Despite the
seemingly ominous message of those objects, he claims, "I find it very
easy to work here – it's very quiet and peaceful."

CARMEN MARC VALVO

The Safari room is the designer's favorite in the Central Park West apartment in New York City he shares
with his partner, Christian Knaust, because, he says, "it best reflects my eclectic style." That's putting it
mildly—the designer has somehow successfully mixed an Arts and Crafts–style Stickley sofa with
framed antique Kuban loincloths (hanging above and also used to make throw pillows on the sofa),
original Tibetan Tiger carpets, and an antique Chinese leather-bound chest used as a coffee table. The
side chairs were originally from the Hotel Knaust, in Sweden, and date to the late 1800s—Valvo had them
recovered in leopard-print calfskin. The coat hanger is a Hans Hoffman piece draped with antique
Masai beaded neckpieces and other jewelry.

STEPHEN DWECK

Stephen Dweck has said he's known for the unexpected. So it was no surprise that when he bought a house on the Jersey Shore, his philosophy of interior design was anything but beach-house chic. The jewelry designer, whose home base is Brooklyn, gutted the house, stripping it down to its Victorian roots, but keeping original architectural details such as moldings and hardware. Then he added paint—the dining room is bright blue, the living room, deep red, a guest room is coral, and the master bath is purple to match the Bergdorf Goodman shopping bag (the designer was originally an art student). It got even more interesting when Dweck and his wife, Sarise, started buying furniture. One room has vintage Bertoia chairs and a neon chandelier; another, Indian silver chairs and a chinoiserie screen. He describes the finished product as "an amazing piece of jewelry."

Opposite This is a beach house? Dweck upholstered the 19th-century settee in the living room with dress fabric and jeweled studs. The chairs are antique Chinese, and the walls are painted Smoldering Red from Benjamin Moore.

STEVE FABRIKANT

Some couples acquire small summer homes with all sorts of additions in mind. But to Steve Fabrikant, enlarging a 1970s, eight-hundred-square-foot Westhampton, New York, cottage made no sense. Instead, the designer, who trained as an architect, chose to turn the two-car garage into a summer kitchen. His wife, Nancy, thought it was crazy but ultimately fell for the unconventional arrangement. The garage faces the swimming pool, providing the perfect spot for summer entertaining, and the renovation was fairly easy. Walls were whitewashed, a farm table was added, and, of course, the ultimate guy toy, a Chicago Combustion (now known as Lazy Man) barbecue, was procured.

Below The two-car garage has a Dutch door and traditional garage doors. Half of the driveway was set with paving stones and grass; the other half is gravel. *Opposite* Doors lead to the pool area that Fabrikant has expertly landscaped.

CHERYL FINNEGAN

It seems fitting that the designer of an accessories line called Virgins, Saints & Angels would choose a colonial Mexican town, with its cobblestone streets, spectacular churches, and Catholic culture filled with iconography, as her base of operations. Cheryl Finnegan had left a husband and a high-powered image-consulting job in San Francisco to come to San Miguel de Allende for a six-month yoga retreat—a way to regroup and rethink her future. In the eight years since, she started designing accessories and built a successful business, had a daughter (Tallulah), and remarried (to the pop artist Jaime Shelley Tovar). The family home, which is still a work in progress, is a compound of three separate houses—the youngest dates to the 1940s—with a total of five bedrooms. Set on a hilltop, it has views of the town square below and the Bajio mountains in the distance. Rather than combining all three houses, the Illinois native hired set designer–turned–architect Theresa Wachter to make it work. "The secret is that you don't remember where the outdoor ends and the indoor begins," says Finnegan.

Top left and opposite bottom far right A fishpond is home to goldfish, koi, and a special species of fish that eat mosquitoes. *Bottom left* Each bedroom has an attached kitchenette so guests can take meals at their leisure. *Opposite top near right* The chandelier, which burns candles only, is made of tin and can be lowered using a pulley. *Opposite top far right* The home's exterior is constructed of stone, polished concrete, copper, local ceramics, and mesquite wood. *Opposite bottom near right* One of the five bedrooms.

ISTVAN FRANCER

Istvan Francer isn't exactly a household name, but as the creative designer for Theory he is in the enviable position of being exceedingly popular and relatively anonymous at the same time. The weekend home that he shares with his partner, John Cummins, is in a corner of northwest Connecticut and dates to the 1740s. The couple bought the house, which sits on seven and a half acres, six years ago. The appeal was twofold: It had been renovated by the previous owners, who installed a kitchen with top-of-the-line appliances, and there was plenty of room for a substantial garden (Cummins is a caterer and an event planner). They lost no time filling the retreat with an eclectic mix of furnishings that include a modernist sofa by Antonio Citterio, various pieces from the more traditional Le Décor Français showroom, and selectively placed taxidermy.

Above A bison head watches over the entry, alongside a set of antique architectural engravings and a collection of straw hats. *Right* A painting by Yugoslavian artist Istvan Szajko hangs in the master bedroom above a chair and an ottoman by Williams-Sonoma Home.

NICK GRAHAM

There are those who buy California ranch–style houses and use them as a base upon which to add layers, like a cake. Nick and Margot Graham, however, are not among them. The founder of JOE BOXER and his wife, an artist, exercised relative restraint in renovating their sixty-year-old, three-thousand-square-foot structure in Marin County. That's not to say they didn't make changes. Architect Andrew Fischer was called on for both the practical (raising the floors and ceilings) and the aesthetic (maximizing views of the trees and streams surrounding the property by adding outdoor decks). And while it's not obvious, the home has many green touches, including solar panels on the roof, siding made of plantation-grown renewable pine, low-voltage fixtures, and windows in place of central air conditioning.

Above Upholstered sofas and chairs in the living room were custom made; the wood-armed chair is by Alvar Aalto, and a Robsjohn-Gibbings coffee table sits on a cowhide rug. Margot's art hangs on the walls. *Opposite top* The Grahams' house is clad in the same material that sculptor Richard Serra uses—the metal develops a rustlike patina over time. The work of another artist, Damien Hirst, hangs inside, while Butter, Graham's golden Lab, keeps watch outside. *Opposite bottom* A salvaged floor joist was the starting point for the dining room table, designed by architect Andrew Fischer and surrounded by vintage Danish chairs.

JOHNSON HARTIG

Johnson Hartig chose his 1920s home, which he describes as "Mediterranean bungalow" in style, because of its proximity to his office. Los Angeles traffic is legendary, and the designer of Libertine admits to suffering from road rage, so a short commute to the office from home is mandatory. To walk through the two-thousand-square-foot, three-bedroom home is to take a journey through various styles that somehow all work together. Delightfully colorful and anything but minimalist, it is filled with a curated clutter of collections that range from the unexpected (such as Staffordshire porcelain dogs) to the fashionable (works by Damien Hirst). Hartig studied painting and drawing and later worked as an assistant to an interior designer, which may explain his very studied use of color (down to the painted white floors) and seemingly perfect placement of furniture and objects. He says that the houses he admires most are a mixture of new and antique, and admits to loving the English Country and Americana styles. They're seemingly contradictory, but with Hartig's magic touch they come off as completely complementary.

Above Hartig designed the bed and set it against chocolate brown walls. The screen was bought at auction; it once belonged to the legendary American designer Geoffrey Beene. *Opposite* Spin art by Damien Hirst hangs in the living room, which has a massive Lucite coffee table.

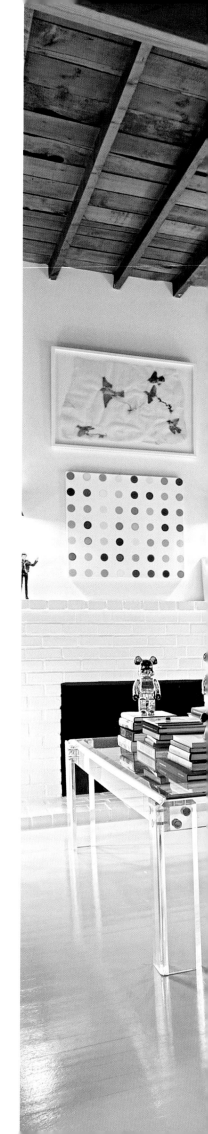

CAROLINA HERRERA

Almost every item in Carolina Herrera's home has an illustrious past. The Venezuelan native, known for her quietly elegant designs, lives in a town house filled with heirlooms (many are museum quality) from both her family and that of her husband, Reinaldo, along with art galore, including family portraits by Salvador Dalí. It's over-the-top in a refined and elegant way, befitting a woman who has mingled with royalty and dressed Jacqueline Kennedy Onassis. The 1850s Upper East Side residence was purchased twelve years ago, after the Herreras became empty nesters, save for Gaspar, their black poodle. While the couple didn't use a decorator, they did get expert advice from friends in that field, including John Stefanidis, Kenneth Jay Lane, and the legendary Chessy Rayner. The Herreras frequently retreat to La Vega, Reinaldo's family estate in Caracas, but this is the couple's only home in New York. They do not weekend in the Hamptons, or elsewhere, and Herrera has often said that she "would not, could not" think of living anywhere else.

Opposite The designer believes that everyone looks good in a red room, which might explain the color she chose for her vast drawing room. This desk, a Louis XV–era antique, is strategically placed in a light-filled area.

Below The designer's dining room is decorated with matching topiaries (they are rotated so the sunlight hits them evenly) and looks out onto more greenery in her garden. An 18th-century Italian table and the 19th-century French dining chairs around it were purchased specifically for this space from the Chinese Porcelain Company in New York. *Opposite* The home boasts six fireplaces—this one is in the Blue and Yellow Sitting Room. The furniture around it is a combination of 18th-century family heirlooms and upholstery from George Smith. A horse painting by John Frederick Herring, Sr., the official animal painter of British royalty in the 1800s, hangs to the left of the fireplace.

ROD KEENAN

You'd never know from looking at it today, but the 1885 Harlem town house that Rod Keenan has lived in for a decade had actually been abandoned for 30 years when he bought it. "The Castle," as it is known, now houses both his studio and his showroom, along with living spaces for himself and two roommates, after undergoing a gut renovation. "Only the facade and footprint of the property remain," he says. Which explains the staircase, shown here, decidedly different from the usual, ornate town house staircases of that era. This particular section leads down to his studio and up to the parlor level, which houses the drawing room, the kitchen, and the dining room. It is lined with photos of his millinery creations as featured in various magazines.

REGINA KRAVITZ

For 24 years Regina Kravitz has been lucky enough to live in this architectural wonder, designed by the architect Preston Phillips, in Southampton, New York. She was drawn to this house overlooking Shinnecock Bay because of "the panoramic view, the bluffs—cliffs are something unusual in the Hamptons." Today the fashion designer–turned–image consultant uses it as a place to "garden, cook, kayak, read, write, cycle, entertain friends, and dream."

TOMMY HILFIGER

Tommy Hilfiger has always followed his instincts, from the time he decided he'd rather go into retail than go to college, and especially when it came to building a home. When he heard a plot near his land in Greenwich, Connecticut, might be coming up for sale, he pounced. A year and a half later, he moved into Stone Hill, his Georgian-style mansion. The design was influenced by the White House, yet the furnishings are anything but presidential (with one exception: the basketball court). Instead of the formality one might expect, Hilfiger opted for a relaxed elegance that reflects multiple interests and eras (his last home was filled with furniture from the Duchess of Windsor's country château). He enlisted interior designer Cindy Rinfret, who decorated his last nine homes, for this twenty-thousand-square-foot project as well. There are the luxurious touches such as Hermès furniture and cashmere walls, a full spa with steam room, and a state-of-the-art cinema. But there's also the pure fun, like the basketball court, tennis court, squash court and billiard room. In a sense, this home is the ultimate representation of the Hilfiger brand—masculine and elegant with the right touch of Americana and a healthy dose of rock and roll.

Top Hilfiger poses with his wife, Dee Ocleppo, and his Bentley at the entrance to their Connecticut home. *Bottom* The designer has a collection of about 50 works by Andy Warhol. This one, of Mick Jagger, was signed by both the artist and the subject. *Opposite* The master bedroom is all about luxurious materials—a fur throw on the bed, walls upholstered in cashmere—and there's always a roaring fire on cold winter nights.

Below The bedroom of Hilfiger's son Richard has an all-American theme. *Opposite* The aptly named "Adirondack Room" is anchored by a fieldstone fireplace adorned by an Austrian mirror. A painting of the flag by Hilfiger's daughter Ally hangs to the left, and suspended from the ceiling is the requisite antler chandelier.

SWAIM AND CHRISTINA HUTSON

"When you have two kids, you gotta get serious," said Swaim Hutson of the decision to move to Cobble Hill, Brooklyn, from Manhattan a year ago. His wife, Christina, was about to give birth to their son, Valentine, and they already had a two-year-old daughter, Lowe. Space was an issue. In Brooklyn, the couple (who have their own label, Hutson) was able to rent two floors in a town house with a backyard and a deck. "It's definitely worth it," said Swaim of the move. "We can really enjoy the outdoors here." And he's got more room to both display and expand the duo's collections, which vary according to time and mood—their current obsession is wall clocks. Overall, Swaim describes the vibe in his home as modern hippie. "Christina comes from more of a hippie side, and I come from more of a prep side," he explains. "But preppy hippies don't really exist." They do now.

Right and opposite top Their current obsession is clocks of all kinds— from quirky contemporary to vintage. *Opposite bottom* The couple collects books on design, photography, and art.

BETSEY JOHNSON

It's hard to believe, but Betsey Johnson painted her New York apartment white before she thought better of that idea. Nobody familiar with the designer's colorful, whimsical, and feminine aesthetic could picture the woman dubbed fashion's "original wild child" in a minimalist white space. It lasted all of two weeks. She picked up a can of pink paint, and the rest, as they say, is thankfully history. Not surprisingly, the result is an explosion of pink, her signature color. What is surprising is how she managed to create a strikingly sophisticated space dominated by a color that is more often associated with Barbie than anything else. Johnson combined her avid love of flea markets, garage sales, and antiques shops with her uncanny sense of design to furnish her eighteen-hundred-square-foot loft on lower Fifth Avenue (she also has homes in East Hampton and Zihuatanejo, Mexico). It's a wonderful mix of old and new, with just the right amount of carefully curated clutter. "Fill your house with stuff you love, because I believe they all go together if you personally love them," she says. "Old, new, antique or super-modern, whatever makes you happy when you come home."

Top left The designer in her loft, where there is plenty of room to turn cartwheels, which is her signature move at the end of her fashion shows. *Bottom left* Like the designer, the kitchen is anything but conventional. The decor was centered around an industrial zinc sink with a marble backsplash. *Opposite* In the dining room, vintage Knoll chairs by Warren Platner sit at an antiques table set under a chandelier found at an antique shop. Silk roses add the wink-wink touch emblematic of Johnson's designs.

DONNA KARAN

Donna Karan has said she's happiest in Bali and Africa, but both places are a bit too far from her New York City base to realistically get to on a regular basis. But at just three hours away, the Turks and Caicos Islands in the Caribbean were perfect. The designer and her late husband, Stephan Weiss, had renewed their wedding vows at Parrot Cay shortly after the thousand-acre private island resort opened. She later bought land on the island, and hired a team of architects that included Cheon Yew Kuan (who designed the Begawan Giri resort in Bali) and Bonetti/Kozerski Studio (who designed her New York City and Hamptons homes) to create her island compound, which was completed two years ago. Six structures sit on the beachfront site: a main house (with an original Balinese teak pavilion on top), two guesthouses, a pavilion, and a spa house complete with steam bath. There's also a yoga hut (Karan practices daily) that was originally built in Bali, then disassembled and shipped to Parrot Cay and rebuilt in a place of honor on the beach.

Top left Karan's yoga hut has 360-degree water views. *Bottom left* A teak sofa is covered in natural brushed cotton canvas; the graphic woven throw is from Africa, as are the headrests on the coffee table. Windows are shaded by split bamboo roll-down screens with breezy natural muslin curtains. *Opposite top* All the furniture, including the teak dining table, benches, and armchairs, was custom designed by the team of architects. *Opposite bottom* An infinity pool, lined with volcanic stone from Bali, is set on top of the main house to maximize sunset views. *Following pages* The living area of a guesthouse features a rattan ceiling and cedar wood walls. Sliding doors open onto a pool deck.

JENNI KAYNE

"I like to call this my modern barn," says Jenni Kayne of the home she shares with her husband, Richard Ehrlich, their son, Tanner, and two French bulldogs, named Mr. Jack and Yoko. "We bought an Amish barn in Pennsylvania and had all the wood brought over here. So all the wood in the house is reclaimed." It took more than two years to make the 1980s Beverly Hills structure liveable. "We gutted it, took it down to the studs," she says. They just moved in last year, and Kayne is quick to point out items that are still missing. But overall the home, located in a neighborhood where the young (she launched her line seven years ago at the tender age of 21) designer says "all the families live," seems to express the same vision she has for her clothing: refined with a bit of an edge.

Right Kayne's kitchen is her favorite room in the house. *Below* Native American paintings in the living room are by Alison Van Pelt. *Opposite* The entry to Kayne's house in the Beverly Hills Flats. *Following pages left* The table at the bottom of the staircase was purchased from the decorator Barbara Barry, who had it in her home. *Following pages right* A large soaking tub from Waterworks is the focus of the master bathroom, which looks out onto a bamboo garden.

RON CHERESKIN

On the surface, it wouldn't seem that the illustrator and fashion designer Ron Chereskin would have much in common with Halston besides, of course, the business. But Chereskin and his partner, Howard Goldfarb, spend summer weekends in a Fire Island house once owned by the legendary fashion designer. "There's a lot of wood and its almost like being on a boat," says Chereskin. His idea was to bring the outside in—which he did by putting in large windows with views of the Japanese-style garden on one side and the bay on the other. Inside, there are a few furnishings left over from the Halston days, including a round table from the *Carpathia*, the ship that rescued *Titanic* survivors.

SANDRA MÜLLER

"This place is like a little cottage," says jewelry designer Sandra Müller of her Los Angeles home, where she lives with Titi, her Maltese. The 1920s, two-bedroom house also serves as her design studio and workshop and has enough outdoor space for small dinner and cocktail parties. In this photo, Müller set the table for afternoon lemonade. Everything is vintage (except the bowl, by the artist Yassi Mazandi), from the kilim pillows, the American quilt, and the French country–style chairs to Müller's favorite, a 1940s cotton kilim rug found on one of her many trips to India.

VICTOR COSTA

"This is a room in which to relax, to escape the hustle and bustle of Seventh Avenue," says Victor Costa of his living room, designed (as was the rest of the house) by his partner, Clay Cope. Their 200-year-old home is perched atop a small mountain in the Litchfield Hills of northwest Connecticut, with views of the foothills of the Berkshire Mountains. The living room was strategically separated into three sitting areas and is furnished with mostly French antique pieces and accessories. The chair at left was once in the Hattie Carnegie couture salon, in New York City.

YIGAL AZROUËL

"I didn't decorate my house immediately when I moved in," says Yigal Azrouël of his Chelsea apartment in New York City. "I am always decorating—I love flea markets like the Brimfield market in Massachusetts and the Porte de Clignancourt in Paris." Indeed, the designer's crystal chandelier and curvaceous chaise were Brimfield treasures, and he scored the dining chairs at a New York flea market. His various antique pieces mix well with contemporary finds, including pendant lamps, a mirror, and a coffee table, all from BDDW. But he's still not done: "I recently bought some handwoven rugs from Morocco to add some warmth and color," Azrouël says.

PAT KERR

"I built this penthouse twenty years ago on top of a building that was already there," says Patt Kerr of her Memphis apartment overlooking the Mississippi River. It's somehow fitting that a woman known for bridal gowns would put a box on top of an existing structure—like a topper on a wedding cake. She's got another home, on the ground, called East House in nearby Germantown, Tennessee, that she built about fifteen years ago when she and her husband returned to the States after living in London for two decades. (There, they lived in a John Nash–designed house in Regent's Park.) While she can't remember its square footage or the bedroom count ("My housekeeper died, and she was the one who knew everything"), she calls it her cozy cottage. Both homes are filled with antiques (Kerr is an unabashed Anglo- and Francophile) collected while living abroad. She is especially attracted to angels and any imagery that, to her, conveys love. "Because my world is bridal, I am a consummate romantic, both in my personal life and in my home."

Top left An antechamber in Kerr's East House, decorated for Christmas with antique Santas. The floors are painted concrete, and the etched-glass windows are from English pub doors. *Center left* View of the house from the swimming pool. *Bottom left* Kerr in the drawing room by an antique Aubusson petit point; the chair is covered in Scalamandré fabric. *Opposite* A table in the English-style garden laid for a bridal luncheon with moss and Lady Banks roses.

NAEEM KHAN

"Designing a home is like designing a dress. I can visualize it," says Naeem Khan. "I architecturally know what to do with a space." And what a space— his SoHo loft is fifty feet wide and one hundred feet long, with full floor-to-ceiling windows on two sides. Naeem met his wife, Ranjana, a former model, when he worked for Halston, and they need the space because they love to entertain. It is not uncommon for the couple, whose first date was at Studio 54, to host parties for as many as two hundred people. There's an open living area with a huge tufted ottoman that can be used as seating or a surface for plates, and a dining area with a table that is a whopping fourteen feet long and forty-six inches wide. "We removed a window, shut the street down, and had a crane bring it up," Naeem remembers. "Just last week I had a dinner for eighteen people. We were all at that table, and it was amazing."

Below Khan met Andy Warhol while working for Halston; he bought the shoe prints directly from the artist. *Opposite* The loft is divided into distinct areas for entertaining. The dining table is made from one solid piece of Indonesian mahogany.

BLAKE KUWAHARA

The eyewear designer Blake Kuwahara describes his Sausalito, California, home—with its custom-painted ochre exterior and Spanish tile roof—as "very South of France." Built in 1931, the home sits on a verdant hillside, framed by redwood trees and with a view of Angel Island. With his partner, Lars Toftdahl, Kuwahara has owned this home for fourteen years and decorated it with flea market finds from around the world (London's Portobello Market and the market at Isle-sur-la-Sorgue in Provence are favorites).

Left The breakfast nook opens up to the front garden of the house. *Below* The living room is a United Nations of design, with a De La Espada sofa from London, candlesticks from Milan, a throw pillow from South Africa, an oil painting from Denmark, and a 19th-century limestone fireplace from France. *Opposite* The formal dining room doubles as Kuwahara's office space, with an antique French farm table, a Fortuny pendant lamp, and views of San Francisco Bay.

DEREK LAM

"I wanted the apartment to be a mix of California beachy casualness and urban New York simplicity," says Derek Lam of the home he shares with his partner, Jan-Hendrik Schlottmann. The apartment, not far from Lam's SoHo boutique, is a penthouse that looks like a small house dropped on top of a classic cast-iron building in SoHo. The designer grew up in San Francisco, which explains his melding of bicoastal styles and attitudes. To help channel his vision of "West Coast casual with classical notes," Lam called on James Scully, who has produced his fashion shows for years, and is a skilled interior designer as well. Scully assisted with both the layout of the space and the often daunting task of choosing paint colors that would complement but not compete with the couple's furnishings. The two areas that Lam had under his own control were the wraparound terrace and interior winter garden. "It's the first 'room' upon entering the apartment, where I keep my jasmine and dogwood trees from October until April," he explains.

Top left Lam, who is the creative director of Tod's in addition to running his own label, with his partner, Jan-Hendrik Schlottmann. *Center left* Lam bought the antique French farm table in 1992 after receiving his first paycheck from Michael Kors, where he once worked. The Dennis Hopper photograph of the Paris skyline reminds them of the house Jan sold to fund Lam's label. *Bottom left* Old meets new in the living room, with Cappellini sofas and 18th-century French chairs. Paintings are by the Brooklyn artist Jim Lee. *Opposite* Lam wanted a "cozy and mysterious" bedroom and went for deep green walls and a dark brown Le Corbusier chaise. The bookcase was custom made in pale cedar (which Lam calls a beachlike accent).

RICHARD LAMBERTSON
AND JOHN TRUEX

Richard Lambertson and John Truex chose this Sharon, Connecticut, weekend house for two distinct features: a barn and a tennis court (they play every Sunday morning). The duo, who founded their eponymous firm twelve years ago, believe Phelps Barnum designed the stone-and-wood home amid the greenery of nine mostly wooded acres. It's a short drive from their New York City base, where Lambertson, who was once the design director for Gucci Group and had the vision to hire Tom Ford away from Perry Ellis, is currently the vice president and design director of leather accessories for Tiffany & Co. (Truex holds the same title at the esteemed luxury retailer, which bought their company in 2009.) When in the country, Truex likes to relax and read or ride the horse he stables nearby, while Lambertson can be found tending to the gardens. He also co-owns Privet House, a home furnishings and antiques store with two locations in Connecticut. Needless to say, Lambertson loves shopping (what better excuse than to say it's for the store?) and is prone to impromptu re-arranging. As luck would have it, at the time of this writing, the duo's new apartment in Manhattan is under renovation with the bulk of the decorating awaiting his magic touch.

Top left The couple can sit side by side in their home office, at a desk they designed. An antique apothecary cabinet is used for storage; the swing-arm lamps are vintage factory fixtures from Lambertson's shop, Privet House. *Center left* Outdoor spaces were designed by Michael Trapp, an antiques dealer who also has a garden design business. *Bottom left* The dining room is a marriage of periods and styles, with 1950s chairs covered in raffia-grass fabric, a French chandelier, and mix-and-match vases on a classic Belgian linen tablecloth. *Opposite* A once low-ceilinged room became a lofty library, and a favorite spot in the house. The tension wires are load bearing, and a dramatic 19th-century French mirror hangs above the ornate mantel; the 1930s club chairs are also French and the sofa is by Ralph Lauren Home.

LIZ LANGE

As a mother of two and the owner of a successful fashion business, Liz Lange didn't have much time to decorate her new apartment. The creator of chic maternity wear had, with her husband, Jeff, sold their previous place and decided, for the time being, to rent an apartment on the thirty-second floor of what she calls an it-is-what-it-is 1970s building on Manhattan's Upper East Side. There's only so much one can do with a rental, and Lange didn't want to do much with a place she didn't actually own. So she called on her old friend, the groovy product and interior designer Jonathan Adler, to help. He suggested staining the parquet floors a dark ebony and painting the walls white, then set about giving the place some personality. Furnishings came from her old apartment and Adler's store, and empty spaces were filled after an intense two-day, all-over-town shopping extravaganza.

Above Vintage chairs and an inlay side table hold court under a wall of framed vintage *Vogue* covers. *Opposite* Adler used a screen of his own design to create an entryway where there wasn't one. A zebra-print cowhide rug adds a graphic touch, and the Indian peacock mirror a dash of glamour.

RALPH LAUREN

Ralph Lauren has spoken many times about his commitment to authenticity and preserving heritage. If you didn't believe him before, one look at his multiple-dwelling ranch in Colorado will change your mind. The land was originally settled by homesteaders in the 1800s, and several buildings on the sixteen-thousand-acre spread outside Telluride remain, with names like Little Bear, Little Brown, and Little Blue Pony. It was a one-hundred-year-old barn that sold him on the place, but the rest of the Double RL Ranch was built from scratch—a four-bedroom main lodge and three guestroom "tepees." Lauren now spends the month of July here (he also owns homes on Fifth Avenue; in Bedford, New York; in Montauk, Long Island; and in Jamaica). The interiors are like walking into a giant Double RL store, and in places it's hard to distinguish the old from the new, and the manufactured from the handmade. The Bronx native, whose parents emigrated from Belarus, seems to have singlehandedly created what many now consider a distinctly American interiors style, and he's clearly living it out West. But he's not done—Lauren has said that this ranch is still a work in progress.

Top left Guests dream of staying in one of the trio of tepees on the property, despite the fact that they are not heated. *Center left* Ralph Lauren rides the range in a jeep. *Bottom left* A view of the San Juan Mountains from the pool. *Opposite* The holiday table is set with Double RL Ranch logo plates and Ralph Lauren Home flatware and linens. *Following pages* The Laurens mixed several period styles in this large log cabin–style room. Mission-style chairs by Stickley mingle with leather club chairs around a dramatic stone fireplace, and Tiffany-style lamps sit on twig tables. *Following pages left* The master bedroom in the main house is a style homage to the 1800s, when this land was first settled. Above the bed hangs a Native American blanket from that era that looks like an American flag; concho belts, also from the 19th century, are hung on either side of the bed. A collection of Native American blankets is stacked at the foot of the bed, on a vintage chest. *Following pages right* This small cabin next to the paddock is used as a tack house.

HENRY JACOBSON

Henry Jacobson's northern California home, The Lodge, dates to 1920, when it was built as a summer residence for a wealthy industrialist. It's in a gated community and set on lush grounds (with a pool, a spa, and a rose garden) at the foot of Mount Tamalpais, which can be seen from the family room, shown here. Jacobson designed all the upholstery for the room himself and had it made by Matt Stoich, a furniture maker based in Larkspur, California. The rest of the space is a mix of cultures—from Egyptian (the rug) and Moroccan (the chest in the alcove) to Chinese (the altarlike chest at the window) to the Fortuny silk pendant lamp that the designer bought in Venice and calls his personal favorite.

ROBIN RENZI

Robin Renzi, of Me & Ro, had a lifelong dream of living in an old farmhouse. This 1850s property in Brookhaven, New York, (formerly the home of the noted photographer Alice Boughton), is the realization of that dream. "This is my favorite part of the house," she says of the screened-in porch. The couch and 1930s bamboo folding chairs are both from yard sales; the Swedish hanging lamp, an eBay find; and the ottoman, from a shop in Greenport, on the North Fork of Long Island. It makes for a very serene spot where, the designer says, "I have sat for hours and hours reading, designing, watching the birds, and sitting in the hammock doing absolutely nothing."

MONICA BOTKIER

Monica Botkier left her native Brooklyn at age 17, vowing to never return. But, three children later, she and her husband, Dean Moodie, are back, in a 100-year-old brownstone in Fort Greene. It was three years from purchase to move-in (a gut renovation was involved), but the finished product is a modern interpretation of turn-of-the-century style with the help of Spacesmith architects and the interior designer Valerie Pasquiou. The only original item in the entrance area is the staircase railing—stairs, doors, moldings, and even that brick wall were all added.

127

NANETTE LEPORE

Robert Savage first noticed the 1849 Italianate Manhattan town house while walking his daughter to school. It seemed too expensive so he never said anything about it to his wife and business partner, Nanette Lepore. But six months later, she spied the same West Village building. It was still for sale, and the price had been lowered. The couple bought it. The previous owner's style was "stuffy," and Lepore's was decidedly more modern, so the renovation involved making the spaces architecturally simpler. The Ohio native then hired Jonathan Adler to give the place a personality while, he recalls, "leaving room for dancing." The strategy was to render the walls and floors fairly neutral while infusing lots of bold color through furnishings—a mix of Adler's own pieces, vintage modern furniture, ethnic accents, a touch of Hollywood Regency, and accessories from Lepore's various collections. The result is eclectic and glamorous, a grown-up home for a woman who, at age nine, created an outfit for a neighbor out of a floral bedspread and a beaded choker.

Right The marble mantel in the living room survived the renovation; above it hangs a painting of Eva Peron found at a flea market. The glass ship chandelier is antique, one of many in Lepore's extensive collection.

Right High ceilings make for grand window treatments, with Manuel Canovas viscose-linen fabric, which complement the Lepore-designed area rug, from Doris Leslie Blau. The chairs in the foreground are by Warren Platner for Knoll, and the Butterfield sofa is Adler's own design.

MICHAEL LEVA

It was not love at first sight for Michael Leva and the 1765 saltbox that is now his weekend home in the Berkshire Mountains in Massachusetts—even after he'd bought it. But once Leva, who is the senior vice president of design at J.Jill, painted the entire house in various shades of light gray, and created what he felt was a symmetrical look, he started to like the small (seventeen hundred square feet) house a lot more. It took two years of renovating just about everything except the wide elm-plank floors, but Leva finally had a place to house all of his treasured antiques that had been languishing in a storage space. And he was finally, truly, in love.

Left The lap pool was painted to look like a pond, algae and all, and Leva, an avid gardener, added the plants. *Opposite* In a sunlit corner of the guest bedroom, Leva placed an antique Czech desk and a 1950s Danish klismos-style chair. A Swedish schoolroom chair (*foreground*) is stacked with poetry journals and vintage decorating magazines.

MARCELLA AND JOHAN LINDEBERG

"We have moved twenty-three times in thirteen years," says Johan Lindeberg. "We are nomads. Many of the pieces in our home have been around the world with us." He and his wife, Marcella, seem to have settled down (for now) in a four-story building in Greenwich Village that functions as a live-work space. The founder of J. Lindeberg left last year to start a new label, Paris 68, and to launch a consulting business that counts Justin Timberlake's William Rast brand among its clients. The live-work situation is a bit unusual. The house the Lindebergs live in with their daughter, Blue, is a former sign factory, and their studio is in the building next door, so they connected the two with a staircase. Lindeberg reveals that although he designed furniture earlier in his career, none of it is in their current home. It's a work in progress, and he gives all the credit to his wife, but says, "I think we're both pretty good when it comes to interiors."

Top right A staircase connects the dining area to the couple's studio in the building next door. Marcella's photographs of kick boxers hang on the brick wall. *Bottom right* The glass dining table once belonged to fellow CFDA member Norma Kamali. The chairs are a flea market find, and the art was created specifically for the space by Johan's niece, Emma Bernhardsson. *Opposite* Overlapping rugs lie under a Vladimir Kagan sofa, a Warren Platner chair and ottoman, and a groovy chaise in the double-height living room.

ELIZABETH LOCKE

The jewelry designer Elizabeth Locke and her husband, John Staelin, are only the fourth owners of Clay Hill, an 1816 Federal-style house in Virginia horse country. The six-thousand-square-foot home, with three-foot-thick walls, was built by former Hessian POWs (German troops who fought for the British Empire against American colonists), and is surrounded by seventy acres of farmland, complete with cows, horses, and a henhouse. Locke, who grew up in the Shenandoah Valley, says she always wanted to live on a farm and, for more than thirty years, she has (her office is conveniently located just ten minutes away). The couple bought the property as newlyweds in 1979 and admit they took their time—OK, decades—renovating and decorating. The furniture, mostly English antiques, with Oriental carpets as accents, is well-suited to the overall style and period of the home. Over the years there's almost nothing they haven't done to the place, while keeping its charm—and one bathroom with lime-colored fixtures that date to the 1920s—intact.

Above The house and grounds are near Civil War battle sites. *Opposite top left* Riding boots are kept just inside the front door. *Opposite top right* The guest room features a hand-carved four-poster canopy bed, clad in Anichini linens and Clarence House toile fabric. *Opposite bottom* Locke's favorite color is gray, the color of the entryway. The antique bench against the staircase was a wedding gift.

TINA LUTZ

To some couples, moving to a residence a mere subway stop outside of Manhattan is the equivalent of living in another country. But Tina Lutz and her husband, Justin Morris, took moving a three-hour train ride and two states away in stride. When their son, Lou, was about two years old, they decided to make their Kingston, Rhode Island, weekend house, with its surrounding forty-two acres, their primary residence. As self-described architecture geeks, the couple says the house was inspired by the legendary architect and furniture designer Marcel Breuer, and is filled with mostly vintage modern furniture. Morris has his office there and Lutz works three days a week at the Lutz & Patmos studio in New York City, staying at their old one-bedroom apartment. With this arrangement, Lutz says she feels like she has the "perfect city-country balance."

Top left Lou frolics on the lawn with his dad, Justin Morris. *Center left* A built-in banquette is the perfect perch for enjoying the fireplace. *Bottom left* Tina Lutz in a guestroom with an installation by the French artist Fabrice Langlade. *Opposite* Lou's room has a wall of framed family photos and, of course, a mini gallery of his own work.

SALVATORE CESARANI

Salvatore Cesarani married for love, but one wouldn't be faulted for wondering if perhaps real estate had something to do with his attraction to his wife, Nancy, as well. The couple's current home—a coveted Brooklyn brownstone—was built in the 1900s by Nancy's grandmother. Located in Park Slope, the house has a generous backyard filled with greenery. "We thought the addition of climbing ivy was a perfect frame for this piece," says Nancy of the stone sculpture hung on the couple's cedar fence.

MARK EISEN

It is hard not to envy the life of the South African designer Mark Eisen and his wife, Karen. This shot, for example, was taken at Normandie, his wine farm in Franschhoek, just outside Cape Town. The property was one of the original 27 French Huguenot wine farms that were established in 1693 and is the culinary version of a national treasure. Their kitchen features a locally made table and chairs, set underneath modern hanging pendant lamps by Tom Dixon. From this spot, the Eisens have breakfast, host cozy dinners, and have beautiful views of the Groot Drakenstein mountain range.

DEBORAH LLOYD

Deborah Lloyd wakes up to the sun streaming through her bedroom windows and the birds chirping in the garden just beyond. The creative director and co-president of Kate Spade makes her home in an 1860s Brooklyn brownstone she shares with husband, Simon Arscott, and their dog, Harry Winston Churchill. A fireplace original to the house centers the room, which has an impressive array of art including a Man Ray sketch and a photograph by Horst, along with a surprising but fun splash of bright fuchsia, thanks to a satin quilt the British-born designer bought in Notting Hill years ago. "I love the feeling of 1940s glamour and femininity in this room," she says. "[It] has all my favorite things in it."

SCOTT STERNBERG

One would hope that anyone who calls his label Band of Outsiders would live in a place that was, well, a little outsider-ish. And Scott Sternberg doesn't disappoint. His living room has a wall created by stacks of books, enlivened by a grouping of trolls—the collectible dolls with rainbow-hued hair. "They live on top of the books," he says. "I call them my coven of trolls."

JENNA LYONS

Renovations can be tough on families. While Jenna Lyons, creative director of J.Crew, and her husband, Vincent Mazeau, an artist, were resuscitating what was left of a 19th-century brownstone in Park Slope, Brooklyn, they lived in Mazeau's art studio on the far West Side of Manhattan with five other people, a dog, and two cats. The renovation lasted more than two years; for the last eight months of it Lyons was pregnant and sleeping on a loft bed, just a few feet from the ceiling. It sounds like a nightmare but, Lyons says, it was worth it. The house, after all, needed a lot of work. "We got in over our heads," admits Lyons. "It was either do this and make it what we want, or buy into someone else's renovations that never quite fit what we were looking for." Their son, Beckett, was born two weeks after they moved in. It was hot and the air conditioning wasn't yet working, but it was home.

Above Jenna Lyons with Beckett, now three. *Top left* A cast-iron tub is the star of the master bathroom; the light fixture is mouth-blown glass by Niche Modern. *Bottom left* Wood from old barns and an original tin ceiling give the modern kitchen a rustic accent. *Opposite* The living room chandelier was designed by Lyons and Mazeau and made from old crystals. A George Sherlock traditional sofa is updated with bright yellow fabric. *Following pages left* One of the home's original four bedrooms was converted into Lyons' closet (the sofa and chandelier are both vintage). To be fair, Mazeau has a small closet room of his own. *Following pages right* One of the original mantelpieces is in Beckett's room, along with a mini Verner Panton chair. The walls double as chalkboards and the ceiling is painted with yellow and white stripes.

BOB MACKIE

He's known for his flamboyant creations for supercelebs and stars, but there's nary a feather or sequin in Bob Mackie's homes. There is, however, an abundance of color. The library bar was painted a denim blue, a perfect backdrop for a selection of Indonesian and Mexican masks from his vast collection. A photograph of his longtime client Cher sits on the side table. In his favorite room, the rainbow-bright sunroom, the award-winning designer, who says he "hates beige," poses in front of a wall featuring various works of art including his own painting of the Pointer Sisters, several Dutch lithographs, and works by the artist Bob Kane.

Above The library hosts a display of Indonesian and Mexican masks.
Opposite The sunroom, which also doubles as a TV room, features a kaleidoscope of artwork.

CATHERINE MALANDRINO

Catherine Malandrino is a glamorous woman with an equally glamorous apartment—but not in a particularly glamorous neighborhood. In a city in which your zip code doubles as a social ID, the überchic, French-born designer chose not to reside downtown, or in a hip Brooklyn walk-up, or an Upper East Side status apartment, but on the (upper) Upper West Side. "I need an open horizon in front of me," she explains. "Here, I can see the [Hudson] river, and I have great light. And my son can play stickball and basketball." The loft where she lives with her partner, Bernard Aidan, is, like her collections, full of interesting shapes, textures, and lots of color (because she finds white-box apartments uninspiring). There are classics from well-known artists and designers, but also unsigned pieces that she's picked up at flea markets or auctions—and a few surprises as well. At first glance, a photo in her boudoir area appears to be a fashion shot of a beautiful woman, but upon closer inspection one sees that the subject has tears in her eyes. "This image is about emotion, and for me, it's inspiring," says Malandrino. "It's all about liberating energy." Which could be her motto for decor, fashion—and life itself.

Right The sofa is a Piero Lissoni design for Cappellini; above it hangs a photo of New York City that Malandrino (*above*) scored at an auction of items from Penn Station.

Above Photographs that inspire the designer on display in her boudoir.
Opposite Malandrino says the bookshelf is one of the most important pieces
in her home. "It's my wall of inspiration, my window on the world," she
explains. The bright books stacked on the shelves are photo albums; she
makes a new one every year. The furry orange ottoman is by Paulo Haubert,
and the yellow chair in the background is by Christophe Pillet, who also
designed her boutiques.

ROBERT MARC

He had already purchased a town house and spent two years renovating it when Robert Marc went to a party at a friend's apartment in a Richard Meier–designed building and decided that glass-box living was the life for him. So he bought a two-bedroom, three-thousand-square-foot apartment on the tenth floor of one of the now-iconic towers in New York's West Village and, less than nine months later, moved in. "I wallpapered the TV room and painted the powder room but otherwise made no major changes, as it was designed by an architect I highly admire," explains the eyewear impresario. His restraint is admirable, and it extends to his philosophy of decor as well. Marc enlisted the interior design firm Luxe Studio to help furnish the light-filled space. "Rather than go the obvious route, using slick and extremely modern contemporary furnishings throughout, I decided to mix inviting soft furnishings with the clean and graceful lines of modernist Italian designers of the 1950s and 1960s," he says. He also created a decidedly modern, perhaps even futuristic, master remote control—from which he can adjust lighting, the audio-visual system, heating, air conditioning, and even the window shades. Because people who choose to live in glass houses still need their privacy.

Right The TV room has gorgeous views of the Hudson River and downtown Manhattan. The sofa, chair, and ottoman were custom made; the floor lamp is a vintage design by Gino Sarfatti. Eirik Johnson's *Untitled (tunnel)* C-print graces the wall.

Top left A 400-square-foot terrace runs the length of the living room and is anchored by a sculpture that Marc's designers found in England. *Bottom left* This corner of the TV room features a midcentury table lamp and an iron-nail wall sculpture from the 1970s. *Opposite* The entrance to Marc's bedroom is graced by a bronze sculpture thought to be American from the 1970s. It spins on its base so Marc can "set it according to [his] mood."

LANA MARKS

"Palm Beach is, to me, the ultimate place in the world to live and raise children," says Lana Marks of the city that has been her home for almost thirty years. Originally from South Africa, the luxury handbag and accessories designer has a five-thousand-square-foot three-bedroom condominium with ocean views, in which she raised her two children, now grown. Being surrounded by nature is important to her. Even her office, located nearby on Worth Avenue, has views of the ocean. When she and Neville Marks, her husband, first bought the apartment, they thought it would be temporary, as they owned land nearby where they planned to build a house. "But this is such hassle-free living—the grounds, the pool, the spa are all so exquisitely maintained that we gave up the idea of having a house," says the designer.

Right Marks designed everything in her living room and had almost all of it made in Italy. The one exception is the Lucite coffee table, with a base she sourced stateside and a smoky surface she had made to top it off.

STEVEN STOLMAN

While you can't tell from his dining area, Steven Stolman can host 100 for cocktails at his Palm Beach one-bedroom condo with a 700-square-foot terrace. For more intimate affairs, the designer seats guests in the dining area of his 1,100-square-foot space. The table is a simple, 48-inch round "clothed to the floor with gusto," and set in high-low style, with candlesticks from Pottery Barn and a Revere bowl. But the chairs are the real story here: "They're my absolute most precious furniture, bought at a rummage sale in Southampton," says Stolman. "They belonged to the late, great Nikki Amey—a true Park Avenue eccentric."

KOI SUWANNAGATE

Every morning Koi Suwannagate, her husband, Richard Warburg, and son, Ben Limsumalee, have breakfast at this table in the kitchen of what the designer calls her Spanish modern home in the Silver Lake neighborhood of Los Angeles. Both the table and the chairs around it are from Design Within Reach; their minimalist bones are somewhat disguised by handmade cushions and a tablecloth found at a flea market.

NATALIE CHANIN

"This is my dining table, although it doubles as a drawing spot, afternoon-tea spot, computer spot, and sitting and dreaming spot," says Natalie Chanin, designer of the lifestyle brand Alabama Chanin. The Florence, Alabama–based designer built the table herself, after an actual table she borrowed from a church and had used for presentations. It is made of scrap wood and is 14 feet long because that was the length of the boards she and her partner, Butch Anthony, found. She painted it with an eco-friendly, VOC-free paint and voilà! The multipurpose table is now in a special spot: "It is the sunniest corner of the house and my favorite place," says the designer.

GENE MEYER

Gene Meyer's home, in the Belle Meade area of Miami, is a mini compound, with two small houses connected by a patio covered with a striped, pavilion style awning. Both structures were built in 1941 in what Meyer calls Bahamian cottage style. The designer has lived here with his partner, the interior designer Frank de Biasi, for a decade (they divide their time between Miami and New York City). Meyer is known for his use of color, but de Biasi ironically once worked for the decidedly classical minimalist architect-designer Peter Marino and has said that his current clients "prefer beige." But when it came to decorating these houses on Biscayne Bay, it seems the duo found common ground. The rooms shown here—the living room, the dining room, and the "Florida room"—are in the "front house." The "back house," where Meyer says they "really live" when they're in town, has the master bedroom, the bathroom, and the sitting room. There's no such thing as a white wall here, and the interior colors, the decor, and the layout often change. But one thing is constant: "The house is surrounded by a ten-foot hedge," says Meyer, "so every view is green."

Above The "Florida room" has a sofa that looks built-in but isn't. "We found it at a local shop, and it fit exactly in the space we wanted," says Meyer. The inlay table is Moroccan but was bought in the States. *Opposite* The scalloped edge around the ceiling is made of shells (with a starfish in the center of each) that were hand-painted and hand-glued by Meyer. The table, from Crate & Barrel, got a few coats of paint to brighten it up, as did the chairs. Meyer designed the rug.

One of the designer's favorite objets d'art in his home is a gray bird, by the artist Peter Schlesinger, on the table. That table, a Karl Springer design, is from the couple's old apartment in New York City. The scalloped edge on the shelving is "all over the Caribbean, mostly in the town houses and small cottages," according to Meyer, who also designed the rug in this room. Of note are the plaster-relief sea horse sculptures above the fireplace—they're made from original 1940s molds—and the 1950s sofa, decorated with pillows from Bergdorf Goodman.

Above and right The tenth-floor living room affords southern and western views of New York City. Both sofas are from Edra: One is set with two vintage chairs (*above*); the other floats in front of three African ladders (*right*). The coffee table (*above*) is a classic Eero Saarinen design, and the rug was custom designed by Hani Rashid/ Asymptote to fit the space; its texture is reflected in the mirrored column. *Opposite* Miele's substantial rooftop deck has minimal landscaping but maximum views of sunsets over the Hudson River. Almost all the furniture is from DEDON, including the sofas and the leaf-inspired chaise; the hourglass-shaped Prince Aha side table is a Philippe Starck design for Kartell.

CARLOS MIELE

"My idea was to buy a town house," says Carlos Miele of his original shopping list when it came to creating a home in New York City. "But I need the sky, the view, and the sunset. So I found a little town house on top of a building, and I have all of that, plus the moon." And he bought it: two floors in the modern-yet-appropriate addition to a historic building in Chelsea, with the added bonus of being able to see his store from his rooftop terrace. Originally, the three-bedroom space was "a lot of small rooms," which clearly would not work for a man who "did not want walls." Enter Miele's best friend, the architect Hani Rashid (his firm is Asymptote Architecture), who also designed the aforementioned retail boutique. "He helped me with everything—from the architecture to the furniture," says Miele, creating a style that is "timeless but also looking forward."

NICOLE MILLER

Nicole Miller has lived in TriBeCa for almost thirty years, decades before the area (Triangle Below Canal) boasted hotels owned by the likes of Robert De Niro and restaurants such as Nobu. The neighborhood is known for loft buildings much like the one where Miller lives with her husband, the investment banker Kim Taipale, and their teenage son, Palmer. Over the years she has combined three lofts to create her current three-thousand-square-foot penthouse filled with French and American furniture (mostly reproductions) from the Rhode Island School of Design graduate's favorite postwar decade, the 1960s. It's got a downtown vibe, to be sure, but with a restraint more associated with uptown. Interestingly enough, the designer has described herself as both. Miller also identified with a variety of artist friends, which accounts for her collection that includes works by Andy Warhol and Damien Loeb.

Top left The designer relaxes on a sofa in front of a painting by Damien Loeb. The tiger-stripe throw pillow is her own design. *Center left* A painting by Ellen Gallagher hangs in the living room, where Miller placed a Vladimir Kagan sofa in a happy shade of blue next to a Buddha head she bought in Hong Kong more than 20 years ago. *Bottom left* The fur throw on her bed was once a coat; the painting above it is by Mac James. *Opposite* In the living room area, a set of Le Corbusier furniture (sofa and chairs) sits on a vintage rug; a splash of color comes via the red lacquer cabinet by Jean Prouvé.

MARK BADGLEY AND JAMES MISCHKA

There are many New Yorkers who live in small spaces in the city, only to escape to "real" houses on weekends. Mark Badgley and James Mischka are no different. Their Manhattan apartment is all of 546 square feet in an entirely unsexy part of town that is close to both their office and the route they take to get to La Guardia Airport. Four years ago, the duo ditched their house in the Hamptons for a horse farm in Kentucky and, unless they are working, they go there every weekend—it's just two hours flying time versus (often) double that to get to the Hamptons during the peak summer season. Unlike their city "glass box in the sky," their Kentucky home is a 1920s limestone Dutch colonial–style house that sits on fifteen acres, some of which was cleared to create room for paddocks and rings for Badgley's three horses (he competes). Moon Stone Farm, as it's called, was renovated with most of the original spaces kept intact but modernized in utility and style. The color palette was kept to black and white. Like so many other fashion designers who work with color all day long, they claim to be uncomfortable with color in their homes. Animals are another story—Badgley has said that most horse people come with dogs—and all design plans kept the habits of furry friends in mind.

Right A Restoration Hardware table is set with Hermès china and antique Windsor chairs.

PAUL MORELLI

Paul Morelli is known for elegant, and often intricate, jewelry designs set tastefully with diamonds that he creates in Philadelphia in a building that once was home to his father's theatrical costume company. The designer and his wife, Anne Marie, live in a historic section of the city that dates to the eighteenth century, but on weekends they escape to Solebury, a small town in Bucks County, to a home they bought fifteen years ago as a retreat. The four-acre parcel is surrounded by nature—it abuts a stream, an orchard, and a horse farm—and has a main house and an outbuilding that Anne Marie has dubbed the "summer cottage." Built around 1948, the small cottage is used as both a design studio and a sweet place for summer entertaining.

Right Anne Marie Morelli in her vast yard, preparing for a summer luncheon with friends; the property's cottage is in the background.

GELA NASH-TAYLOR

She always wanted a crest—so much so that when Gela Nash-Taylor started (with her partner Pamela Skaist-Levy) the line Juicy Couture, the logo was designed with two dogs holding a shield that framed their initials, topped off by a crown. Royal aspirations for a girl from Texas, but not unattainable—she married rock royalty in the form of Duran Duran's John Taylor and, as these photos attest, she did get her castle. Technically a manor house, South Wraxall Manor dates to the early fifteenth century and sits on 830 acres, about two hours outside of London. To appropriately outfit a home with this pedigree, Nash-Taylor hired none other than Robert Kime, the go-to interior designer for England's royal set (he is by royal appointment to the Prince of Wales), along with Patrick Kinmonth, an art director, stylist, and set designer with experience in both fashion and theater. It's a win-win situation that has resulted in a manor full of period-perfect pieces. The couple spends most of the year there, inviting friends from around the world to join them (the manor has nine bedrooms) in enjoying English country life.

Below Cricket, anyone? Yasmin Le Bon (left) looks on while Nash-Taylor gets a lesson from her husband, John Taylor. Her son, Travis Nash, is in the background. *Opposite* A guest bedroom has antique Louis XVI canopy beds, upholstered in the original fabric, and walls covered in a print from Braquenié, a French fabric house that dates to the early 1800s.

Top left A table set in a covered arcade is surrounded by bergère chairs with carved frames; the chandelier above is a 19th-century Italian antique. *Below left* There are peacocks on the property in both animal and topiary form. *Below right* Nash-Taylor has two children from her first marriage—her daughter, Zoe, is in the enviable position of claiming this vast room as her bedroom. Flowered antique fabrics frame the windows, Oriental carpets cover the floor, and a massive fireplace provides warmth to combat the damp English weather. *Opposite* At just 5-feet-2-inches tall, the lady of the house can easily submerge her petite self in the ample claw-foot soaking tub. It's placed beneath an antique Venetian mirror and a chandelier dripping with crystals.

ALBERTUS SWANEPOEL

The South African-born designer Albertus Swanepoel seems to accessorize the New York City apartment he shares with his partner, Eddie Marquez (and Pookerdoodle, their cat), with the same attention to detail and creativity he displays in his millinery creations. The foyer, shown, is a perfect example, with a 1970s mirrored credenza and a cork lamp, both found on eBay. African items such as the Ewe dolls mix with a print by Vladimir Tretchikoff and coral from Marquez's native Hawaii.

JOHN WHITLEDGE

Having an apartment above a service station isn't something most people would want, unless, of course, that station services classic cars and is in a building that is a protected landmark in Laguna Beach, California. Such is the life of John Whitledge of Trovata fame, who with his wife, Manuela, scored a two-bedroom apartment, with ocean views, in a building locals call The Boathouse. "I love running down to the beach for a quick surf or for a relaxing read on the sand," he says. "Afterwards, I feel like I just came back from a nice vacation."

ROBERT DANES

If one must live and work in the same space, it helps to have an inspirational view. And boy, does Robert Danes have views. This one, for example, faces west toward the Hudson River and New Jersey beyond, framing incredible sunsets. From the living room and kitchen of the spacious loft in downtown Manhattan, the family (wife Rachel, daughters Azalea and Aurora) can observe the setting sun. There's plenty of room for Danes to design his line of sculptural and modern dresses, along with his new ready-to-wear line, while his girls stage ballet performances and dress-up parades (thanks to a recent chest of vintage "treasures" sent from their grandparents in Texas). Danes is a native Texan; a skull he found on a neighboring ranch as a kid has traveled with him over the years. An old butcher's table is paired with a vintage garden chair.

JOSIE NATORI

Josie Natori knows interiors. The sixty-two-year-old investment banker–turned-designer has overseen the renovation of three homes: a sprawling full-floor apartment in New York City, a country house, and a pied-à-terre in Paris, shown here. It was the first apartment she saw, and it was dark—not what she pictured for her place in the City of Light. But it was off the Avenue Montaigne in the eighth arrondissement (where her "neighbors" would include the Champs-Élysées, the Arc de Triomphe, the Place de la Concorde, and the Paris Opera) and so, on impulse, she bought it. It took five years and the skills of the legendary interior designer Jacques Grange to turn the twelve-room, 19th-century home into the light-filled, elegant space that Natori had always dreamed of. Most furnishings are antiques, and there are silk fabrics everywhere—framing curtains, covering walls, and, of course, on furniture. She says it's "not stiff," but it's definitely decorated. No matter. Natori has said she needs Paris for her soul, and here, she has it.

Bottom left The columns were added by Grange. A Steinway piano sits in the background; Natori *(top left)* is an accomplished pianist. She was a soloist with the Manilla philharmonic as a child and has also played at Carnegie Hall. *Opposite* In the library, chairs are upholstered with a flame-patterned fabric designed by Grange and sit on a Kashan rug. Walls are upholstered in Fortuny fabric.

Below The salon has a mix of styles—from a marble bust to a lacquer
table inlaid with mother-of-pearl. *Opposite* 17th-century Portuguese
paintings hang in the dining room.

VANESSA NOEL

Vanessa Noel has perhaps one of the most glamorous live-work spaces going. Her boutique takes up the entire first floor of her home, and her showroom, part of the second floor of the Upper East Side town house she bought in 2001 and spent a whopping seven years renovating. "The layout of the space was very important, so that work and residence could be separated and linked when desired," she explains. The house dates to 1899, and Noel, who studied fine art and architecture at Cornell, was intent on preserving the period details—or creating new ones, like the Lucite doorknobs and period-perfect moldings she custom-designed and had installed throughout the house. "A house is like a cupcake," she says. "And I'm all about the icing."

Left A 17th-century Russian chandelier hangs in the entry hall over a classic black-and-white marble floor. The mantel was shipped from Copenhagen, and the mirror above it was purchased at auction stateside. *Opposite* All eight fireplaces in Noel's home are functional. The horse on the mantel is a Chinese antiquity that's more than 2,000 years old. Walls were painted a color that mimics her stretch alligator boots. The chandelier was bought at auction—from the home's previous owner—and the table and chairs are American antiques.

JOHN PATRICK

"My decorating philosophy is a hybrid of High Dutch meets Elsie de Wolfe meets the [modern painter] Charles Sheeler meets a little bit of Shaker," said John Patrick of the home he shares with his partner, Walter Fleming. The previous owners of the 1820s farmhouse in Columbia County, New York, were dairy farmers and there were rooms with dirt floors—there was much work to be done. The hat designer—turned—poster child for stylish sustainable clothing painted the place himself and sourced furniture that was either antique or made locally. "I've filled up this house four times and four times sold it all," he admits.

Above Patrick, at right, with Walter Fleming. *Top left* New nailheads and vintage cotton fabric breathe new life into an antique wing chair. *Bottom left* Patrick painted the 1820s home himself, but hired local carpenters to make all the doors. *Opposite* A raffia tassel that Patrick had made in Indonesia dangles seductively over the antique soaking tub.

TOM AND LINDA PLATT

Some American designers work with color all day long and want serenity at home. That is not the case with Tom and Linda Platt, whose Park Avenue one-bedroom apartment is awash in citrus hues. While many might find the abundance of in-your-face shades of lemon and lime a tad aggressive, Linda says that she finds it incredibly soothing. It's no doubt an irreverent choice for an apartment in a New York City building that dates to 1924, but the Platts are not known for subtlety. They chose furnishings that are sculptural and colorful, with a splash of pattern thrown in here and there via cow-print chairs, a Giò Ponti cabinet covered with Fornasetti images, and surprises such as the yellow and green painted logs in the fireplace.

Below left The television and other electronics are hidden in a vintage plywood cabinet. *Below right* The table is set with dinnerware by Marek Cecula (a ceramic artist who used to have a shop in SoHo) and flanked by chairs by Dialogica upholstered in shades of pink, purple, and yellow. *Left* The architects Peter Stamberg and Paul Aferiat designed the walls with niches for displaying objects. A red Dialogica sofa anchors the living room; the coffee table is by Noguchi.

LAURA PORETZKY

An art-filled West Village apartment in New York City is where the designer Laura Poretzky, her rock star husband, Diego Garcia (formerly of Elefant), and their French bulldog, Alaia (named after the designer), make their home. "My other passion, besides fashion, is the decorative arts," she admits. Her tastes tend toward vintage modern, as evidenced by the Milo Baughman chairs and the Knoll sofa in her living room. The couple also collects art—a Hope Atherton painting and a mixed-media piece by Donald Baechler hang in the living room *(below)*; a Russell Young painting of Elizabeth Taylor hangs above a 1960s Plexiglas console in the bedroom *(right)*.

TRACY REESE

Tracy Reese thinks beige is boring. And you won't see much of it in the clothes she designs or the apartment she lives in, either. Color—lots and lots of seemingly casually thrown together shades, but in reality very carefully chosen—reigns on her runway and in this Midtown Manhattan co-op, complete with a sunken living room. The apartment represented a rebirth for the designer, who had spent a decade in her previous place and associated its furnishings with her college years. Buying her own one-bedroom made the Detroit native feel more grown up, and the decor needed to reflect her newfound sophistication. An expert scavenger, Reese frequented flea markets and secondhand stores for pieces with good bones, treasures that would find new life after a coat of paint or a change of upholstery fabric. They now commingle with other finds from online sources, catalogs, and local stores, against a backdrop of brightly colored walls. It's all finished with a touch of kitsch—in moderation, of course—which Reese believes every home needs because it adds personality.

Top right The designer perches on an antique chaise she had reupholstered; she also made the curtains. *Bottom right* A double mirror found at a flea market hangs above Reese's bed, which was ordered from the Ballard Designs catalog. *Opposite* An antique red armoire is set against an equally red wall that's been stenciled with a gold fleur-de-lis pattern.

LELA ROSE

Street-level apartments are traditionally undesirable to city dwellers, yet Lela Rose actually prefers them. "I love living on the ground floor," she admits, "even though people come by and think we're a store." The Texas native bought her TriBeCa loft more than five years ago and hired WORK Architecture Company (architects who had worked for Rem Koolhaas) to design the space—which might surprise those familiar with her decidedly feminine fashions. The result is an ultramodern, minimalist three-level loft. "I wanted to be able to have one hundred people at a seated dinner, or just the four of us, without moving things around," says Rose. And she got it—the ground floor is a series of spaces delineated by color and materials, from gray felt in the game room to aubergine in the kitchen to white resin in the entryway. Each area functions separately, but are designed to connect via a fifty-five-foot-long table in four sections, used for those large dinners or to function as a catwalk. "This is not your normal New York apartment at all," she admits. "But it so fits the way we live."

Top left There's a terrace outside the master bedroom; this space used to be indoors. *Bottom left* A bamboo Shaker-style "box" room was originally intended as a bar area, but Rose says her family eats dinner here most nights. *Opposite* The entry room floor is white resin (Rose says, "You practically have to walk with a Swiffer behind you"), an eight-piece sectional by Pierre Paulin circles the column, and the Louis XIV chair was a gift from her mother.

Above To seat one hundred guests, the living room table descends from the mesh ceiling, a Shaker box table comes up from the floor, the dining room table gets extensions, and a game table in the media room will connect to the remaining tables, according to architect Amale Andraos. *Opposite* An opaque resin "tunnel" connects his-and-her closets.

CYNTHIA ROWLEY

It should come as no surprise that Cynthia Rowley's home, like the women's wear she designs, is sophisticated and feminine, with touches of whimsy. The designer bought the 1845 Greek Revival town house in New York City's West Village five years ago. At the time, it was divided into individual apartments so a gut renovation was required to make it the perfect home for the Illinois native, her husband, Bill Powers, and their two daughters, Kit and Gigi. It's also a mini gallery. Her husband was once the editor of *BlackBook* magazine and is now a novelist, an artist, and a gallery owner (with partners Andy Spade and James Frey). The couple's choice in art is informed and a tad eccentric—their collection reads like a Who's Who of contemporary art, with pieces by Ryan McGinness, Elizabeth Peyton, Will Cotton (who did a portrait of Gigi), Rachel Feinstein, Yoshitomo Nara, Rob Pruitt, Takashi Murakami, Richard Prince, and Tom Sachs. There's another typical Rowley touch: a baby grand piano, fitted with an insulated, plastic-lined body that can be used as a cooler for various beverages. As with many New York town houses, the facade exudes historic sophistication, but the back is where the action is. Rowley's is no different. Her kitchen and dining area are walled in glass and open directly into the backyard. In this city a backyard is a green luxury, and a water feature (usually a fountain) is considered glamorous, but a lap pool, like the one Rowley added, is a rarity.

Above The designer and her husband, Bill Powers. *Opposite* Rowley's Resort 2009 collection presentation took place poolside, amid vintage lounge chairs and a tree swing.

CHRISTIAN ROTH

The eyewear designer Christian Roth has a heck of a view from the terrace of his weekend home in the historic 14th-century village of Ramatuelle, France. Roth, with his partner, Eric Domege, bought it six years ago as a getaway from their home in Monaco. "The view is towards the legendary Pampelonne Beach," explains Roth. "We love the peacefulness of the town, yet we're so close to the buzzing St. Tropez summer life."

JASON WU

Jason Wu lives in a modest one-bedroom apartment with a very simple color scheme: gray. To be fair, there is some color in his bedroom, namely the wallpaper, which he says feels "lush, cozy, and intimate." The Taiwanese native got the side table at an antiques store and dressed it up with a seashell lamp and an alarm clock that was a gift from his father. He's had it since junior high school, and it remains a favorite.

CYNTHIA STEFFE

It took four years before Cynthia Steffe found a country home to her liking. The Sioux City, Iowa, native says that because of her Midwestern roots, she prefers the country to the beach. And rural she got—the closest town to her Catskills home has a population of just 222, and the property is surrounded by 45 acres of mostly wooded land. The house has become a repository for items the designer has collected over the years. Most are antique, like the game boards that adorn the living room walls, the McCoy, Weller and Roseville pottery, the twee English plates, and the bird's nests.

RACHEL ROY

"It's a great, family-friendly neighborhood," says Rachel Roy of her decision to buy two apartments in TriBeCa that she then combined with the help of architect Thomas Juul-Hanson. She lives here with her two daughters, Ava and Tallulah, and Ava's Maltese, named Puppy. "Because I am constantly surrounded by colors, prints and fabrics at work, I like my apartment and my bedroom to be as clean and sparse, yet as comfortable, as possible," explains Roy of her overall design philosophy. "The one thing I cannot live without, besides light, is flowers. I rely on flowers in every room to bring warmth and color into the apartment."

Below Roy's Poliform modernist sofa is strewn with colorful throw pillows, some made from Hermès scarves, and others, from fabrics she found in Ghana while on a trip for OrphanAid Africa. The oversize, industrial-style lamp is from the Wyeth showroom in New York City. *Opposite* A chandelier custom made by Italamp hangs over the wooden dining table that's set with vintage china for a children's tea party. Her architect designed the chairs in a color that would hide marks from messy and sticky hands, and the rocker was a gift from a college friend after Tallulah was born.

RALPH RUCCI

After living on the Upper East Side for more than two decades, Ralph Rucci wanted to move downtown. That is, until a realtor showed this self-described "hippie-bohemian" a one-bedroom penthouse surrounded by a terrace with eastern, western, and southern views. "When I'm here, I don't feel like I'm in a neighborhood. I'm just home," he now says. At first, he painted the walls white and filled the space with Asian antiques and French furniture; he later realized he needed help pulling the interiors together. Enter his good friend the interior designer Susan Gutfreund. "She created an incubator of luxury," he says. "She wanted it to be really sexy, and it is. And she wanted it to be masculine, and it is." Fabrics came from the legendary maison Georges Le Manach. Walls were clad in leather; curtains, embroidered in a pattern that matches the ceiling; carpets, silk and cashmere. All this for a man who lives with a fifty-six-pound English bulldog named Twombly. Because ultimately the apartment was meant to be comfortable and luxurious—a place where it's okay to spill wine or, perhaps, drool on furniture.

Top left A petrified wood stool holds a stack of books. *Bottom left* The bedroom contains a pair of 15th-century Chenet bronzes formerly owned by Hubert de Givenchy. *Opposite* Billy Baldwin bronze bookcases line two of the dining room walls (the third is mirrored). The table is a petrified bronze tree trunk with a glass top and is surrounded by 18th-century Scholar chairs with cushions made from antique obis. Lights were strategically placed above the thatched lacquer ceiling—they cast geometric shadows on the space. *Following pages* Silk velvet from Le Manach was custom colored and used to cover the sofa and chairs in Rucci's living room. Two 18th-century Japanese lacquered dowry chests are used in lieu of a coffee table.

SELIMA SALAUN

Selima Salaun isn't the type of woman who wears flats and, until recently, wasn't one to take the subway either. Her home, therefore, needed to be a four-inch-heel-able walk from her Selima Optique boutiques (there are four in New York). Her SoHo lofts (plural) fit the commute requirements. The Tunisian-born designer bought the first in 1993 and the second, right beneath it, in 1996. She, her husband, Jean-Marie, and their teenagers, Theo and Zoe, sleep, eat, and entertain upstairs; Jean-Marie's music studio, Selima's office, and the TV room are downstairs. Four dogs and two cats roam in between. The furnishings reflect the life and diverse interests of a woman who was born in North Africa, schooled in Paris, and counts Tokyo as one of her favorite places. The two lofts are not directly connected—they are two separate spaces—and the photos shown here are of the "upper level." Best yet, the walls are thick. "When I am dancing upstairs, nobody can hear me downstairs," says the designer.

Below A collection of robots ("I was obsessed," she admits) sits on an Indian cabinet. *Opposite top* Salaun's husband, Jean-Marie, was Antoni Gaudí–inspired when he decided to tile the upstairs bathroom in mosaics.

Bottom left The framed insects were purchased at a store in Kyoto, Japan, as a gift for her son, but "my cats destroyed these. It's so funny how much they hate them." Framed butterflies came from Evolution in SoHo; poufs are reminiscent of her North African roots but were bought locally. *Bottom right* The designer in her living room. The regal purple sofa is an antique; the painting behind it, of the poets Arthur Rimbaud and Paul Verlaine, is by Madeleine Pearson.

ANGEL SANCHEZ

After years of living in a tiny TriBeCa apartment, Angel Sanchez and his partner, the interior designer Christopher Coleman, left Manhattan for twelve-hundred light-filled square feet in Williamsburg, Brooklyn. The duo has lately been collaborating on interiors for private clients and found inspiration for their new home in Latin American pop art from the 1960s and '70s. It's a very colorful departure for the Venezuelan native, as the previous apartment they shared was swathed in subdued shades of black and gray with chrome accents. "I told Chris, 'Be careful. I don't want it to look like a kindergarten,'" he explains. "You've seen my fashion. I like color, but not too many together." In the living room a custom sofa sits in conversation with two re-covered vintage chairs and an outdoor table that found new life indoors with a black Formica top. The centerpiece of the bedroom is a headboard made from fabric stretched over a frame. Wall-to-wall black carpeting camouflages a parquet floor that wasn't to the couple's liking. Sanchez banished the original orange kitchen cabinets for black ones that would better offset the geometric wallpaper, inspired by the Venezuelan artist Alejandro Otero. "This apartment didn't need to reflect my fashion," he says of the finished product. "It just had to be a happy place to live in. The apartment is very graphic. We played with color block and proportions, drawing inspiration from [Piet] Mondrian, Memphis [the 1980s Milan-based design collective], and Latin American pop art."

Right The two vintage chairs were re-covered with interesting fabrics like a graphic rug from Dubai and a bedcover found in the South of France. *Following pages left* A colorful fabric headboard brightens up the bedroom. *Following pages right* Sleek black cabinets ground the kitchen's graphic-patterned wallpaper.

ARNOLD SCAASI

Arnold Scaasi believes that rooms in which one doesn't spend much time can be a bit wild, while those in which one really "lives" should be more subdued. Foyers, for example, Scaasi loves to slather in red, and he has cloaked entryways in several homes, including his own New York City apartment, in that vibrant shade. He calls his decorating style eclectic—and indeed, it is hard to categorize a mix that includes Asian antiques and artworks by his good friend Louise Nevelson, who died in 1988. The designer, who came to New York City in 1954 to work for the legendary designer Charles James, is very picky when it comes to real estate. He prefers a duplex, because it "feels like a house," and he must have a view of either Central Park or the East River. From the living room of this particular duplex—which took two years and more than one hundred apartment go-sees to find—Scaasi and his partner, Parker Ladd, can gaze upon the Queensboro Bridge. Mission accomplished.

Top right The designer's study has blue-and-white toile walls. *Center right* Buddhist statues guard Louise Nevelson's *Vertical Cloud*. *Bottom right* Scaasi and Ladd pose in front of a piece by the French artist Jean Dubuffet. *Opposite* Another study is filled with antiques, including a portrait that reminds Scaasi of his stylish Aunt Ida, who inspired him to become a designer.

RICKY SERBIN

Ricky Serbin is a rock star in the vintage couture world—he collects it and he sells it. His partner, Mitchell Benjamin, an architect, is also a collector, albeit of Biedermeier furniture. And the San Francisco Dutch colonial–style home they share is filled with museum-quality pieces of furniture. (Serbin's office and collections are relegated to a four-hundred-square-foot addition at the rear of the home.) Over the years, Biedermeier has become a passion for both: "The fun of the treasure hunt is one of the joys of our travel together," says Serbin. "We've found pieces in Rome, Milan, Stockholm, Paris, and New Orleans." Their home, purchased ten years ago, was a "hidden jewel waiting to be re-polished into gemstone" in St. Francis Wood, an Olmsted Brothers–designed neighborhood which, according to a poll, boasts the most satisfied people in all of San Francisco.

Above All Biedermeier, (almost) all the time—both the armchair and the side chairs date to 1825. The desk is a Gustavian design from the 1800s, made in Sweden. *Right* Benjamin designed the custom cabinetry to showcase the couple's collection of Lalique pieces—one of which, a 1926 lamp found at the Paris flea markets, hangs from the ceiling. Both walls and floor are clad in tile; the former from Waterworks, the latter, a French marble.

KATRIN ZIMMERMANN

The jewelry designer Katrin Zimmermann spent her childhood summers at this house in the Black Forest in Germany, with views of the entire chain of the Alps—from Austria to Switzerland and France. Zimmermann, whose stateside home is in Harlem, now spends two months of the year here and especially enjoys the double-height living room, with its 5,000-volume library and a Roman statue that dates to the second century. The designer was recently given this house by her mother and looks forward to giving it to her own daughter someday.

CAROLINA AMATO

The dining area of Carolina Amato's Long Island home is chock-full of items the accessories designer, best known for her legendary gloves, has foraged for at antiques stores the world over. The dining table and chairs, for example, are 19th-century American antiques. A hand-blown Murano chandelier was purchased in Venice. Items on the room divider are all antiques—a silver tray with vintage glass decanters, fox candleholders purchased in London, a chinoiserie vase, and a metal basin that now holds wine bottles. Underneath it all, a runner from the designer's scarf collection.

MARCIA SHERRILL

She's known for creating luxurious handbags from exotic skins accented with 24-karat-gold hardware that can fetch as much as $100,000, but when it came to decorating her Upper East Side apartment in New York City, Marcia Sherrill went to Tepper Galleries, the Manhattan auction house, or designed (and often made) furnishings herself. In her bedroom, all the bedding, lampshades, and paintings are her own creations. A Balinese carving is hung over her bed, and a fur rug by Hermès Leather covers the floor.

KARI SIGERSON

"I had my eye on this apartment for a while," said Kari Sigerson, who house-hunted in a very specific, four-block area at the tip of Manhattan. The designer—one half of the accessories duo Sigerson Morrison—bought the three-bedroom space to inhabit with her husband, Dirk Kaufman, their daughter, Eva Belle, and a six-year-old German shepherd named Ursa. Thanks to her business partner, Miranda Morrison, whose brother Jasper is a sought-after industrial and furniture designer, she had (relatively) easy access to fabulous modern furnishings as well. "When we first moved in, I had all sorts of flash ideas on how to make this place jazzy," she remembers. "But after living here for a while, we slowly realized that what we really want is much different from what we originally imagined. We are finally moving forward."

Above Sigerson on one of her two terraces. *Top right* The designer's living room is like a Cappellini showroom: The sofa, coffee table, and shelves are all from the Italian company. *Bottom right* Collections of Rex Ray art on the wall and pottery by Raymor and Eva Zeisel. *Opposite* Jasper Morrison side chairs surround a Saarinen tulip table in the dining room. The sheepskin throws are from Ikea.

PAUL SINCLAIRE

Paul Sinclaire has had a discriminating eye from a young age. He likes to tell a story about spotting a Franz Kline painting at a gallery in Manhattan and asking for it as a fourteenth-birthday present. He got it, and to this day he says it is a cornerstone of his art collection (an impressive one, which also includes works by Terry Richardson, Alex Katz, and David Hockney). Sinclaire, the president and creative director of Tevrow + Chase (and most recently Sinclaire 10), has homes in Miami, New York, and Washington, D.C., which he shares with his partner of twenty-six years, Eric Berthold. But their base is a six-thousand-square-foot, 1920s Georgian home in Toronto. When it comes to decor, the former fashion editor says, "Our philosophy is and always has been steeped in a sense of classicism, like the clothes I have always loved— American sportswear." The home is a tasteful combination of traditional and modern, old and new, with surprising but outlandish accessories, because style, as the designer has been known to assert, is in the soul.

Left The couple with their Brittany spaniels, Stuart, India, and Bea. *Opposite* A Ming dynasty blanc de Chine vase, a late-16th-century Chinese teapot, and a Tang era tomb guard adorn the living room mantel; a painting by the British artist Peter Kinley hangs above it.

AMY SMILOVIC

One look at Amy Smilovic's Greenwich, Connecticut, home and there's no doubt that the founder of the women's wear brand Tibi lives there. Vibrant color and Tibi-esque patterns abound, albeit strategically. But it wasn't always that way. Smilovic and her husband, Frank (the president of Tibi), bought the 1962 Colonial Revival–style home after moving back to the States following a three-year stint in Hong Kong. They lived in it, with their two young sons, for a full seven years before redecorating and making it truly their own. With the help of the interior designer Bruce Shostak (who, upon arrival, ripped down the previous owner's rooster curtains, followed by the red monkey wallpaper), the six-bedroom, fifty-six-hundred-square-foot home was completely transformed in the seven months between spring and fall fashion weeks. And with minimal construction—only one wall was torn down. Ever the fashion designer, Smilovic contributed to the process by creating elaborate mood boards for every room, complete with inspiration photos from interior design magazines and fabric swatches (Shostak says that was a first for him with a client). She also looked to other fashion designers for inspiration—Chloé for the bedroom, Marni for the kitchen. The Georgia native (and art school graduate) designed many of the rugs and some of the wallpaper (inking a licensing deal with the New Orleans–based company Flavor Paper in the process). The result is an elegant but lively mix of pieces she acquired in Hong Kong with custom upholstery, vintage modern designs, and, of course, a massive infusion of color.

Top left Smilovic's dining room chairs are covered in dress fabric. Center left In her home office, Smilovic mixed a vintage bamboo chair with a Parsons-style desk from West Elm. Her then-four-year-old son, Charlie, created the fashionista must-have list that sits framed on her desk. Bottom left The master bath is papered with a pattern by Cole & Son and lit by an antique chandelier. In contrast, the armchair has a sleek modern design. Opposite Smilovic designed the wallpaper in the master bedroom (available through Flavor Paper).

MICHELLE SMITH

When Michelle Smith first viewed her Upper East Side apartment, it had been empty for fifteen years. The two-thousand-square-foot two-bedroom with double-height ceilings and views of the Whitney Museum was owned by the estate of Naomi Leff, a legendary interior designer (with numerous famous and private clients such as Steven Spielberg and Tom Cruise). Leff had died before she was able to move into the space of her own design—and it was in far from livable condition. The electrical system was original (1920s), the plumbing had to be redone, and the kitchen needed updating. A year later, the woman behind the label Milly moved in with her husband and business partner, Andrew Oshrin, and their daughter, Sophia. While she refers to it as a restful environment, the interior, designed by Shaun Jackson, exudes get-noticed glamour thanks to selective touches of gold, sprinkled about in wallpaper, rugs, and dramatic chandeliers. Most of Smith's furnishings are antiques from various eras that somehow harmoniously converge inside this apartment, constructed in the neo-Gothic era. The most modern touch is his-and-her walk-in closets. Smith's has high racks specifically built to hold formal gowns and a wall devoted solely to shoe storage. Which she'll clearly need—the apartment is right across the street from Christian Louboutin.

Above Black-lacquered pocket doors in the living room lead to a jewel box of a dining room. The art deco ebony table looks small but can seat 10 on vintage Gilbert Rohde chairs. *Right* The custom-made sofa is one of the only pieces in Smith's vast living room that isn't vintage or antique; the painting above it, of the author Catherine Millet as a nun, is by the Canadian artist Tony Scherman.

MARIA SNYDER

The model–turned–jewelry designer Maria Snyder lives in a loft in New York City's TriBeCa neighborhood, surrounded by art. She either is the subject or was the creator of most of the works. The eye paintings *(below)*, the posters on the lacquered blue walls *(opposite top)*, and the neon sculpture against the lacquered red wall *(opposite bottom)* were all made by Snyder herself. Not shown here, a portrait of her by Mark Kostabi; the former Yves Saint Laurent model also posed for Antonio Lopez, Alex Katz, Helmut Newton, and David LaChapelle.

KATE SPADE

The renovation of Kate and Andy Spade's Park Avenue apartment, in New York City, took one year, but decorating it took three times as long. It's a classic conundrum for creative types who like to let a room tell them what it wants to be, and to let it grow and evolve over time, much like a collection. And the Spades are avid collectors—of objects, art, people, and ideas. The three-thousand-square-foot three-bedroom apartment interested the couple, who have been together for twenty-five years, because almost nothing had been done to the prewar space for forty years. They did little to alter it—they made one bedroom into a library, added French doors, and did some re-wiring and other basic but ultimately invisible work. After living in a loft, the idea of a series of rooms held great appeal, especially since the two had just become parents. Since that time, there has been a lot of change in their lives. The Spades sold their company (including both the Kate and Jack Spade brands) in 2007. Andy started Partners & Spade more than a year ago and, like the man himself, the new company is hard to categorize: It does some consulting, some branding, and some movie producing. As he likes to say, he has not retired. And for now, Kate seems content to be a stay-at-home mom to five-year-old Bea, extending her brand of cute chic to parenting—she's been known to make her sandwiches in the shape of hearts.

Top right The entry foyer is octagonal in shape and hung with art curated by Andy Spade. *Bottom right* A former maid's room is now a guest room completely covered in Osborne & Little's "Rococo" toile de Jouy wallpaper and fabric. *Opposite* One of Andy's favorite works of art, a drawing by Robert Hawkins that reads "Give me your lunch money," hangs in the living room. *Following pages left* Spade's bar sits atop an antique console table in a corner of the living room. An armchair from Sweden, upholstered in yellow silk brocade, sits in front of it. *Following pages right* In another guest bedroom, the walls are decorated with a selection of found art, hung above an upholstered headboard.

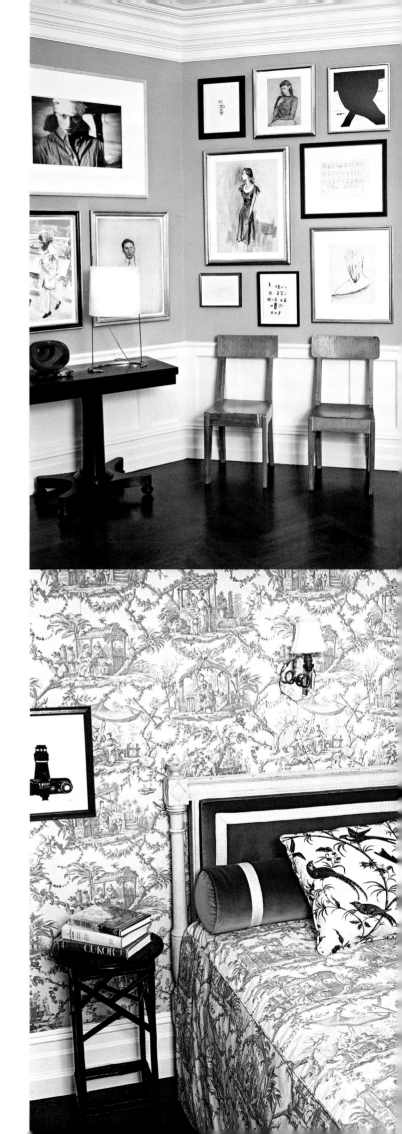

JILL STUART

One look at Jill Stuart's penthouse apartment in the Urban Glass House, in New York City's SoHo neighborhood, the last project by the legendary architect Philip Johnson, and it's hard to believe her previous residence was on the (comparatively) stuffy Upper East Side. This six-bedroom, five-bath space with more than seventy-two floor-to-ceiling windows is all about modernism (as is the architect responsible for the interiors, Annabelle Selldorf) and, of course, the views. From this twelfth-floor apartment, the designer (who lives here with her husband, Ronald Curtis, and their three daughters) has 360-degree views of the city and the Hudson River. Every single element of the interior was meticulously chosen, from the Florence Knoll sofas in the living room, to the impressive selection of art (created by the likes of Julian Schnabel and Willem de Kooning) hung throughout the space, to the Venetian-plastered walls and the oak floor in a chevron pattern. Obsessive? Perhaps. But a home in a Philip Johnson structure requires nothing less.

Below A daybed by the Danish designer Poul Kjærholm is strategically positioned in front of the fireplace in the living room. *Opposite* Annabelle Selldorf designed the dining room table, set with Ted Muehling candle-holders. It sits underneath pendant lamps by the Italian architect Carlo Scarpa for Venini. The painting is by Sue Williams.

ROLAND NIVELAIS

Roland Nivelais says he doesn't understand sports or casual clothes and believes in being polished, groomed, and always prepared. His weekend retreat in Bridgehampton, New York, could be described using the same words. Named Belle Ombre, or Beautiful Shadow, the house, which dates to 1902, is surrounded by century-old Norwegian spruces and maples. The designer's 72-foot lap pool is "reminiscent of a quiet woodland pond." The cottage's interior is filled with antiques from Nivelais's native France and art including his favorite, a small drawing by Jean Cocteau.

SAM AND LIBBY EDELMAN

"Our farmhouse was built in the late 1700s," says Libby Edelman of the Connecticut home she shares with her husband and business partner, Sam. "This room was an add-on in the 1970s to an older part of the house, and we tried to bring the outside into the inside with all the windows." Comfort is key—as evidenced by the Jean Michel Frank–style sofa that seems more beach-chic than vintage modern, with its custom white-denim slipcover. At just under 12 feet, it's possibly the longest residential sofa in the entire state.

CATHY HARDWICK

Her decorator, Mario Buatta, has been called the Prince of Chintz, yet this area of Cathy Hardwick's library remains relatively floral-free. From the comfort of her George Smith tufted chase she can gaze upon the 18th-century Dutch painting she bought in Paris years ago. It is flanked by two Chinese Export jars that sit on gilded brackets; their shape is mimicked by the Berlin jars on the paisley-covered console below.

ELIE TAHARI

Elie Tahari's favorite New York City neighborhood is SoHo, but for years he lived in its polar opposite—the Upper East Side. Yet when he and his wife, Rory (she's the vice chairman and creative director of his eponymous label), toured this triplex penthouse in a former chocolate factory, he immediately knew he'd found their new home. It didn't hurt that the previous owner was the media mogul Rupert Murdoch, who had hired the chic French interior designer Christian Liaigre to work his magic on the ninety-three-hundred-square-foot aerie. As a result, every single item in the apartment was custom designed for the space, even the walnut ceilings. There are five bedrooms (the Taharis have two children, Jeremy and Zoe), a playroom (which had been a workout room), a place for Elie to practice his daily yoga, a master bedroom, generous closets, and two decks with 360-degree views of Lower Manhattan.

Top left The couple sleeps on a Christian Liaigre–designed bed dressed with Matteo linens. *Top right* Cy Twombly's *Roman Notes* hangs behind a piano that was a gift from Rory's mother. It was once owned by the lyricist Martin Charnin, best known as the creator of *Annie. Opposite* The main deck area is 1,400 square feet and has become a favorite place to entertain, especially at sunset.

REBECCA TAYLOR

Rebecca Taylor is a lucky woman—she's one of the only designers featured in this book who did not have to extensively renovate her home before moving in. Which was extra-convenient because she was just about to give birth to twin girls, Zoe and Isabel (she's since had a son, Charlie). The New Zealand native and her husband, Wayne Pate, bought the four-story brownstone four years ago in the family-oriented Park Slope neighborhood in Brooklyn. It was the fulfillment of a dream. Ever since she saw the movie *Moonstruck* years ago, the designer longed for both New York City and a brownstone. She now owns a two-thousand-square-foot, light-filled space with three bedrooms and a generous backyard that has inspired her to explore her green thumb. So far she's planted hydrangeas and rose bushes and, in typical New York fashion, a privacy hedge.

Top left Taylor with husband, Wayne Pate, on the stoop of their brownstone. *Bottom left* A stylish tent makes a nifty fort for the kids to play hide-and-seek in the spacious backyard. *Opposite* Inspirational objects and her kids' drawings create a fun rogues' gallery above a workspace.

Left Pocket doors separate the living areas from the kitchen.
Below Although she claims that she never cooks, Taylor's got
a kitchen worthy of a pro, with Viking appliances and marble
countertops. *Opposite* Twins Zoe and Isabel share a room and a
designer rug by Marni for The Rug Company.

GORDON THOMPSON III

There's a joke in Los Angeles that everybody's house used to be somebody else's, and Gordon Thompson's is no exception—it's where Bette Davis lived from 1968 until her death in 1989. The former executive vice president and creative director of Nike, who successfully revived the Cole Haan brand, bought the West Hollywood apartment after leaving both his job and New York for Los Angeles three years ago. He chose it as much for location as design—from there, he can maintain habits developed in New York City, namely walking to a grocery store, a movie theater, and a coffee shop. The three-bedroom space is a mixture of small and large rooms and, as furnished by Thompson, is filled almost exclusively with vintage modern pieces. "I love designers like Ed Wormley, Tommi Parzinger and Robsjohn-Gibbings because they have the unique ability to combine quality and craftsmanship, all through a modern and clean lens," says Thompson. Indeed, everything adheres to that description except perhaps the chandelier in the dining room, which came with the apartment. "I was going to sell it," admits the designer, "but then I found out that Bette hand-selected it, and it's worth a small fortune." The chandelier, as they say, is staying in the picture.

Top left Thompson's bedroom is anchored by a Ralph Lauren Home bed and has doors that open onto a shaded terrace (*opposite bottom*) from which he has views south to Century City, the Pacific Ocean, and Catalina Island. *Bottom left* Ann Sacks tiles adorn the walls of a small bathroom off the living room. *Opposite top* His living room is a mixture of vintage pieces, including Edward Wormley sofas, an art deco screen, and an Italian gold-leafed coffee table. *Following pages* The dining room furniture is all by Edward Wormley, with the exception of a contemporary rug and an antique Japanese screen depicting the four seasons.

ZANG TOI

If you didn't know better, you'd think this apartment was smack-dab in the middle of a chic Paris arrondissement, not in an old mansion on the Upper East Side of Manhattan. The thirteen-hundred-square-foot one-bedroom is home to the flamboyant Malaysian designer Zang Toi, a Francophile extraordinaire who's been known to fly to Paris for a night—simply to have dinner at his favorite restaurant. He's definitely channeling a lot of Louis XIV in this two-room space, which is filled with many luxurious touches, some more subtle than others. There's the cashmere-covered sofa that's trimmed with mink, a real fur throw rug, an antique Baccarat crystal chandelier worthy of a ballroom, and touches such as high-gloss white walls and a similarly glossy black floor.

Below The designer in his Paris-style apartment. *Bottom left* An antique cabinet is filled with framed family photos. *Opposite* Natasha Zupan's paintings of Marie Antoinette flank a pair of mirrors (one hung in front of the other) above the fireplace in the living room. The chandelier is 19th-century Baccarat, Loro Piana cashmere covers the Louis XVI-style settee, and the rug is luxurious silver fox.

TRINA TURK

Trina Turk has long claimed to draw inspiration from "cocktail party and poolside lifestyle," perhaps because she has not one but two houses—both with pools. On weekends she can be found in a Palm Springs, California, home that dates to 1936 and is known as the Ship of the Desert. But her day-to-day life takes place in the Schapiro house, a 1940 Case Study House in Los Angeles named after the original owners and designed by J.R. Davidson. Although renovations were minimal, decorating was anything but—the designer and her husband, Jonathan Skow, a photographer, are flea market fanatics. Indeed, almost every piece in the home has a past. That hasn't stopped the couple from continuing to shop for things they love, although Turk says "junk is more expensive now."

Below In the wood-paneled dining room of her Los Angeles home, vintage chairs by William Haines are placed around a Herman Miller table designed by George Nelson, with a runner made from a Japanese obi. The terrazzo floors are original to the house. *Opposite* Outdoor furniture on the pool deck is upholstered in a canvas fabric from one of Turk's past collections.

MISH TWORKOWSKI

The town of Millbrook, New York, was settled by Quakers in the mid-eighteenth century. Today it is considered one of the wealthiest areas in the state, with residents that include celebrities such as Liam Neeson and Mary Tyler Moore, along with the highly stylish, such as Mish Tworkowski. The jewelry designer, who was once an in-house jewelry expert at Sotheby's, and his partner, the architect Joseph Singer, bought two acres of land that used to be part of a Victorian-era farm. Singer designed a structure to connect the existing buildings, creating one capacious home. Five years later, new life was breathed into the old barn (now the living room) and the creamery (the master bedroom), and the two-story connector has been finished. Now the whole house looks like it's been there forever.

Left Tworkowski designed the white fences with Moroccan-style arches that surround formal gardens.
Opposite The living room has poured-concrete floors, whitewashed pine walls, and a mix of French and Swedish antiques.

GEORGE SHARP

What could be better than finding a loft whose previous
resident was an architect who had worked for Zaha Hadid?
Such was the real estate karma of George Sharp, the
design director for St. John, who not only scored a space
in what many consider the best part of New York City's
SoHo, but (because of the aforementioned architect) also
got a ground-floor-level, back-of-the-building space
that does not resemble a cave. "The whole back side is
skylights," he explains, "and we have 18-foot ceilings, so
we have incredible light during the day." The sofa in the
living room that Sharp and his wife, Diana, bought in
Germany is flanked by vintage chairs by Harvey Probber
and a Calvin Klein Home coffee table. The "stilts" on
either side support a second level that has two bedrooms
(one is occupied by the couple's teenage son); they're also
flooded with light, thanks to floors of glass block.

MIMI SO

Mimi So says she loves living in Manhattan's Tudor
City because "it's a friendly neighborhood, is within
walking distance of everything, and has great views."
The third-generation jewelry designer has lived here
for five years and chose many custom pieces for her
loft, including the Donghia-upholstered sofa and
chairs shown here. The coffee table has a Frank
Gehry-esque twisted-metal base that looks as if it
could be a piece of jewelry in and of itself.

KEANAN DUFFTY

He's a rocker who has designed clothes for rockers and even a David Bowie–inspired collection for Target. He, his wife, Nancy Garcia, and their three cats live in a loft apartment in the ten-story Morse Building which, when it was built in 1878, was one of the tallest buildings in New York City. Mounted above an antique table the couple bought in London is Erwin Olaf's portrait of Princess Diana from the Dutch photographer's series on dead royalty.

KAY UNGER

It's hard to imagine that a woman who owns more than 150 pairs of shoes would buy a place with almost no storage. Yet that's exactly what Kay Unger did five years ago, when she bought a forty-three-hundred-square-foot loft in SoHo in New York City. It's even harder to imagine that a space that size, which had been recently renovated with a brand-new kitchen and bathrooms (plural), wouldn't have properly designed and dedicated areas for clothing and accessories—the closets didn't even have lighting. But she was in love, and true to the saying, a blind eye was turned and a contractor was hired to create shelves and cubbies. Most of the furniture in the airy space can be described as classic modern, with some vintage pieces or reproductions thrown in for good measure. The designer, who once apprenticed for Geoffrey Beene, introduced color and accent pieces very carefully and deliberately, words that could also apply to her fashion aesthetic.

Above The designer in her studio. *Right* Unger's loft has 15-foot-high walls, making for a very dramatic center fireplace. The bookshelves that surround it were some of the only storage in the space when she bought it. Unger chose upholstery pieces that would maximize conversation—classic club chairs by Edward Wormley and a low, modern daybed upholstered in gold pony.

Above Unger's fashion sketches hang in one bathroom. *Opposite*
The Chicago native chose modern chairs by the architect Mies
van der Rohe (who built several skyscrapers in her hometown) to
put around a traditional-style farm table in the dining room.

DIANE VON FURSTENBERG

Diane von Furstenberg's twenty-seventh-birthday present to herself was a seventy-five-acre estate in Connecticut, on the site of a former tobacco farm. Cloudwalk Farm, as it is called, was secured at a pivotal time in the designer's life—her marriage to Prince Egon von Furstenberg was ending—and she has, in the years since, often referred to it as her "place of refuge." There's a farmhouse, two smaller cottages, and a barn on the land, which was previously owned by a mystery writer. Interestingly, it's the once bohemian-chic, now truly deluxe barn where the ever-stylish grandmother of three and CFDA president actually lives when on the property. And after perusing these photographs, it's not hard to ascertain why she chose the more intimate space (as redesigned by Bill Katz) rather than the larger main house. The most dramatic spot in the barn is a double-height room lined with built-in shelves filled with books and objets d'art collected over the years. Four armchairs by Jacques Adnet, the French art deco—era designer, are strategically positioned in front of the fireplace (the rug underneath is of her own design). Indeed, much of the furniture in the home comes from Paris, where von Furstenberg still keeps an apartment. Other covetable pieces are a dramatic eighteen-foot-long table by George Nakashima and a retractable screen used for movie nights, perhaps suggested by her media mogul husband, Barry Diller. And no sanctuary would be complete without a room for meditation. Von Furstenberg has a marble soaking tub, found in her native Belgium, with a 19th-century painting hung above it, and a lovely antique chaise where she, an avid reader, can devour a tasty tome.

Right The property is filled with several varieties of scented flowers, including roses in a garden just outside the barn and a field of magnolias on the banks of a river that runs through it.

Left Roses and other flowers bloom around the property. *Below left* An antique chaise for reading. *Below* Von Furstenberg relaxes in an art deco armchair by Jacques Adnet. *Opposite* The designer found this marble tub in her native Belgium. *Following pages* The dramatic double-height room features a rug of von Furstenberg's own design.

GARY WOLKOWITZ

Gary Wolkowitz's life was changed simply by walking into the Jil Sander store on the Avenue Montaigne in Paris. "I knew that was how I wanted to live," he remembers. "The stone floor, the plaster walls, the wenge wood, and the stainless steel. It was very disciplined and rigorous in terms of its aesthetic and, at the time, was very advanced." Back in New York, Wolkowitz, the president and design director of Hot Sox, hired the architect of that store, Michael Gabbellini, to transform the thirty-five-hundred-square-foot penthouse that he and his wife, Sarah, had just bought. The resulting space is not typical of a Park Avenue apartment but provides the perfect backdrop for the couple's growing collection of photography. Wolkowitz calls the experience a "marriage made in heaven," and acknowledges that living this simply is not for everyone. "Once you adapt to the rigors of it, it's easy," he claims, adding, "This is about the way you edit your life, rather than how you fill it up."

Right Minimal but interesting furniture in the living room includes a customized Saporiti sofa and chairs that Wolkowitz spied in Tokyo's Hotel Okura. "They never sell them, but I was tenacious about it." Works by Edward Weston, Paul Strand, and André Kertesz are hung via rods on the perfectly white plaster walls.

Below The master bathroom's walls are made of a type of glass that can go from transparent to opaque with the flick of a switch. The marble inside is completely white, with no veins. It is from Yugoslavia, was cut in Carrara and assembled on-site. *Opposite top* A table of brushed stainless steel and glass in the couple's study serves as a vitrine to display photographs and books; that's a Donald Judd chair behind it, and a photograph called *Tumbler* by Aleksandr Rodchenko. *Opposite bottom* A Robert Mapplethorpe platinum print hangs on a black wenge wall above the couple's bed, which is balanced on one single support, creating a floating effect. The bench was made in Greece of pear wood and leather.

PETER SOM

"I wanted an open kitchen," says Peter Som of his recently redone apartment, "but not fully open, because I make a mess when I cook." Som entertains frequently, so getting rid of the former galley kitchen was a priority when renovating his two-bedroom apartment in New York City's West Village. Counters are now Carrara marble, the backsplash is stainless steel, cabinets are a rich cerused oak, and the vintage pendant fixtures can be rotated to focus light where it is needed most—usually in the vicinity of a homemade piecrust, a Som specialty.

MATT MURPHY

"I'm a night owl so the studio-home combination is key," says Matt Murphy of his loft space in the Flatiron district of Manhattan. All but one wall is white, and the rest were ingeniously designed to be convertible—almost everything hides something else. There's a full-wall bulletin board above a full-wall desk and cabinet built in on the left, with an integrated refrigerator, sink, and range. The center island acts as storage, and is movable to open up the space when the accessories designer needs it for meetings or entertaining. "I make art here too," he explains, "so everything is monochrome and movable to accommodate large and small drawings."

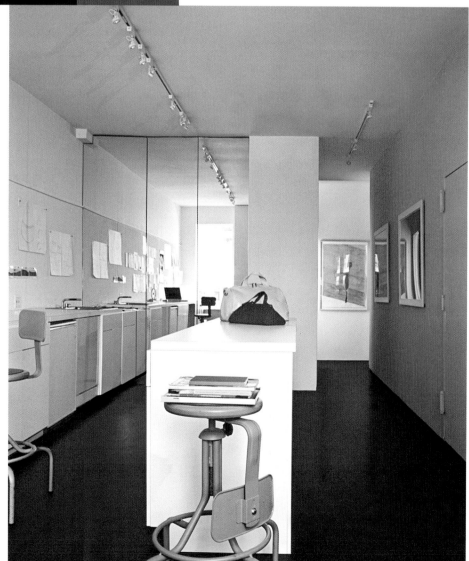

268

ANDREAS MELBOSTAD

"I've lived in Oslo, London, Paris, and now New York," says
Andreas Melbostad. "It is only with this apartment that I decided
to make a home." The designer, who has worked for the likes of
Alber Elbaz, Calvin Klein, and most recently, Phi, furnished his
Chelsea apartment in New York City with favorites by Poul
Kjaerholm, Jean Prouvé, and folding chairs by Armin Wirth.

CURRENT CFDA MEMBERSHIP ROSTER

1	Amsale Aberra	31	Bryan Bradley	61	Michael Colovos
2	Reem Acra	32	Barry Bricken	62	Nicole Colovos
3	Adolfo	33	Thom Browne	63	Sean Combs
4	Simon Alcantara	34	Dana Buchman	64	Rachel Comey
5	Linda Allard	35	Andrew Buckler	65	Anna Corinna Sellinger
6	Carolina Amato	36	Sophie Buhai	66	Maria Cornejo
7	Ron Anderson	37	Tory Burch	67	Esteban Cortazar
8	John Anthony	38	Stephen Burrows	68	Francisco Costa
9	Nak Armstrong	39	Anthony Camargo	69	Victor Costa
10	Brian Atwood	40	Pamela Capone	70	Jeffrey Costello
11	Max Azria	41	Kevin Carrigan	71	Erica Courtney
12	Yigal Azrouël	42	Pierrot Carrilero	72	James Coviello
13	Mark Badgley	43	Liliana Casabal	73	Steven Cox
14	Michael Ball	44	Edmundo Castillo	74	Keren Craig
15	Jeffrey Banks	45	Salvatore Cesarani	75	Philip Crangi
16	Leigh Bantivoglio	46	Richard Chai	76	Sandy Dalal
17	Jhane Barnes	47	Julie Chaiken	77	Robert Danes
18	John Bartlett	48	Amy Chan	78	David Dartnell
19	Victoria Bartlett	49	Charles Chang-Lima	79	Oscar de la Renta
20	Dennis Basso	50	Natalie Chanin	80	Donald Deal
21	Michael Bastian	51	Georgina Chapman	81	Louis Dell'Olio
22	Bradley Bayou	52	Ron Chereskin	82	Pamela Dennis
23	Richard Bengtsson	53	Wenlan Chia	83	Lyn Devon
24	Dianne Benson	54	Susie Cho	84	Kathryn Dianos
25	Chris Benz	55	David Chu	85	Keanan Duffty
26	Alexis Bittar	56	Eva Chow	86	Randolph Duke
27	Kenneth Bonavitacola	57	Doo-Ri Chung	87	Stephen Dweck
28	Sully Bonnelly	58	Peter Cohen	88	Marc Ecko
29	Monica Botkier	59	Kenneth Cole	89	Libby Edelman
30	Marc Bouwer	60	Liz Collins	90	Sam Edelman

91	Mark Eisen	121	Stan Herman	151	Devi Kroell
92	Melinda Eng	122	Lazaro Hernandez	152	Christopher Kunz
93	Steve Fabrikant	123	Carolina Herrera	153	Nicholas Kunz
94	Carlos Falchi	124	Tommy Hilfiger	154	Blake Kuwahara
95	Pina Ferlisi	125	Carole Hochman	155	Steven Lagos
96	Erin Fetherston	126	Christina Hutson	156	Derek Lam
97	Andrew Fezza	127	Swaim Hutson	157	Richard Lambertson
98	Patricia Ficalora	128	Alejandro Ingelmo	158	Adrienne Landau
99	Cheryl Finnegan	129	Marc Jacobs	159	Liz Lange
100	Eileen Fisher	130	Henry Jacobson	160	Ralph Lauren
101	Dana Foley	131	Eric Javits, Jr.	161	Eunice Lee
102	Tom Ford	132	Lisa Jenks	162	Judith Leiber
103	Istvan Francer	133	Betsey Johnson	163	Larry Leight
104	Isaac Franco	134	Alexander Julian	164	Nanette Lepore
105	R. Scott French	135	Gemma Kahng	165	Michael Leva
106	James Galanos	136	Norma Kamali	166	Monique Lhuillier
107	Nancy Geist	137	Donna Karan	167	Phillip Lim
108	Geri Gerard	138	Kasper	168	Johan Lindeberg
109	Justin Giunta	139	Ken Kaufman	169	Marcella Lindeberg
110	Nick Graham	140	Jenni Kayne	170	Adam Lippes
111	Henry Grethel	141	Rod Keenan	171	Deborah Lloyd
112	Jeff Halmos	142	Pat Kerr	172	Elizabeth Locke
113	Tim Hamilton	143	Naeem Khan	173	Tina Lutz
114	Douglas Hannant	144	Eugenia Kim	174	Jenna Lyons
115	Cathy Hardwick	145	Calvin Klein	175	Bob Mackie
116	Karen Harman	146	Michael Kors	176	Jeff Mahshie
117	Dean Harris	147	Fiona Kotur-Marin	177	Catherine Malandrino
118	Johnson Hartig	148	Reed Krakoff	178	Maurice Malone
119	Sylvia Heisel	149	Michel Kramer-Metraux	179	Colette Malouf
120	Joan Helpern	150	Regina Kravitz	180	Isaac Manevitz

CFDA Fashion Award Winners 1981–2009

2009

Womenswear Designer of the Year *Kate & Laura Mulleavy for Rodarte*
Menswear Designer of the Year *Scott Sternberg for Band of Outsiders, Italo Zucchelli for Calvin Klein*
Accessory Designer of the Year *Jack McCollough & Lazaro Hernandez for Proenza Schouler*
Swarovski Award for Womenswear *Alexander Wang*
Swarovski Award for Menswear *Tim Hamilton*
Swarovski Award for Accessory Design *Justin Giunta for Subversive Jewelry*
Eugenia Sheppard Award *Ed Nardoza, Editor in Chief, Women's Wear Daily*
International Award *Marc Jacobs for Louis Vuitton*
Eleanor Lambert Award *Jim Moore, Creative Director, GQ*
Geoffrey Beene Lifetime Achievement Award *Anna Sui*
Board of Directors' Special Tribute *First Lady Michelle Obama*

2008

Womenswear Designer of the Year *Francisco Costa for Calvin Klein*
Menswear Designer of the Year *Tom Ford*
Accessory Designer of the Year *Tory Burch*
Swarovski Award for Womenswear *Kate & Laura Mulleavy for Rodarte*
Swarovski Award for Menswear *Scott Sternberg for Band of Outsiders*
Swarovski Award for Accessory Design *Philip Crangi*
Eugenia Sheppard Award *Candy Pratts Price*
International Award *Dries Van Noten*
Geoffrey Beene Lifetime Achievement Award *Carolina Herrera*
Board of Directors' Special Tribute *Mayor Michael R. Bloomberg*

2007

Womenswear Designer of the Year *Oscar de la Renta and Lazaro Hernandez & Jack McCollough for Proenza Schouler (tie)*
Menswear Designer of the Year *Ralph Lauren*
Accessory Designer of the Year *Derek Lam*
Swarovski Award for Womenswear *Phillip Lim*
Swarovski Award for Menswear *David Neville & Marcus Wainwright for Rag & Bone*
Swarovski Award for Accessory Design *Jessie Randall for Loeffler Randall*
Eugenia Sheppard Award *Robin Givhan, Fashion Editor, Washington Post*
International Award *Pierre Cardin*
Geoffrey Beene Lifetime Achievement Award *Robert Lee Morris*
Eleanor Lambert Award *Patrick Demarchelier*
Board of Directors' Special Tribute *Bono & Ali Hewson*
American Fashion Legend Award *Ralph Lauren*

2006

Womenswear Designer of the Year *Francisco Costa for Calvin Klein*
Menswear Designer of the Year *Thom Browne*
Accessory Designer of the Year *Tom Binns*
Swarovski's Perry Ellis Award for Womenswear *Doo-Ri Chung*
Swarovski's Perry Ellis Award for Menswear *Jeff Halmos, Josia Lamberto-Egan, Sam Shipley & John Whitledge for Trovata*
Swarovski's Perry Ellis Award for Accessory Design *Devi Kroell*
Eugenia Sheppard Award *Bruce Weber*
International Award *Olivier Theyskens*
Lifetime Achievement Award *Stan Herman*
Eleanor Lambert Award *Joan Kaner*
Board of Directors' Special Tribute *Stephen Burrows*

2005

Womenswear Designer of the Year *Vera Wang*
Menswear Designer of the Year *John Varvatos*
Accessory Designer of the Year *Marc Jacobs for Marc Jacobs*
Swarovski's Perry Ellis Award for Womenswear *Derek Lam*
Swarovski's Perry Ellis Award for Menswear *Alexandre Plokhov for Cloak*
Swarovski's Perry Ellis Award for Accessory Design *Anthony Camargo & Nak Armstrong for Anthony Nak*
Eugenia Sheppard Award *Gilles Bensimon*
International Award *Alber Elbaz*
Lifetime Achievement Award *Diane von Furstenberg*
Award for Fashion Influence *Kate Moss*
Board of Directors' Special Tribute *Norma Kamali*

2004

Womenswear Designer of the Year *Carolina Herrera*
Menswear Designer of the Year *Sean Combs for Sean John*
Accessory Designer of the Year *Reed Krakoff for Coach*
Swarovski's Perry Ellis Award for Ready-to-Wear *Zac Posen*
Swarovski's Perry Ellis Award for Accessory Design *Eugenia Kim*
Eugenia Sheppard Award *Teri Agins*
International Award *Miuccia Prada*
Lifetime Achievement Award *Donna Karan*
Fashion Icon Award *Sarah Jessica Parker*
Eleanor Lambert Award *Irving Penn*
Board of Directors' Special Tribute *Tom Ford*

2003

Womenswear Designer of the Year *Narciso Rodriguez*
Menswear Designer of the Year *Michael Kors*
Accessory Designer of the Year *Marc Jacobs for Marc Jacobs*
Swarovski's Perry Ellis Award for Ready-to-Wear *Lazaro Hernandez & Jack McCollough for Proenza Schouler*
Swarovski's Perry Ellis Award for Accessory Design *Brian Atwood*
Eugenia Sheppard Award *André Leon Talley*
International Award *Alexander McQueen*
Lifetime Achievement Award *Anna Wintour*
Fashion Icon Award *Nicole Kidman*
Eleanor Lambert Award *Rose Marie Bravo*
Board of Directors' Special Tribute *Oleg Cassini*

2002

Womenswear Designer of the Year *Narciso Rodriguez*
Menswear Designer of the Year *Marc Jacobs*
Accessory Designer of the Year *Tom Ford for Yves Saint Laurent Rive Gauche*
Perry Ellis Award *Rick Owens*
Eugenia Sheppard Award *Cathy Horyn*
International Award *Hedi Slimane for Dior Homme*
Lifetime Achievement Award *Grace Coddington*
Lifetime Achievement Award *Karl Lagerfeld*
Fashion Icon Award *C. Z. Guest*
Creative Visionary Award *Stephen Gan*
Eleanor Lambert Award *Kal Ruttenstein*

2001

Womenswear Designer of the Year *Tom Ford*
Menswear Designer of the Year *John Varvatos*
Accessory Designer of the Year *Reed Krakoff for Coach*
Perry Ellis Award for Womenswear *Daphne Gutierrez & Nicole Noselli for Bruce*
Perry Ellis Award for Menswear *William Reid*
Perry Ellis Award for Accessories *Edmundo Castillo*
International Designer of the Year *Nicolas Ghesquière for Balenciaga*
Lifetime Achievement Award *Calvin Klein*
Eugenia Sheppard Award *Bridget Foley*
Humanitarian Award *Evelyn Lauder*
Eleanor Lambert Award *Dawn Mello*
Special Award *Bernard Arnault* for his Globalization of the Business of Fashion with Style
Special Award *Bob Mackie* for his Fashion Exuberance
Special Award *Saks Fifth Avenue* for their Retail Leadership of Fashion Targets Breast Cancer

2000

Womenswear Designer of the Year *Oscar de la Renta*
Menswear Designer of the Year *Helmut Lang*
Accessory Designer of the Year *Richard Lambertson & John Truex*
Perry Ellis Award for Womenswear *Miguel Adrover*
Perry Ellis Award for Menswear *John Varvatos*
Perry Ellis Award for Accessories *Dean Harris*
International Designer of the Year *Jean-Paul Gaultier*
Lifetime Achievement Award *Valentino*
Humanitarian Award *Liz Claiborne for the Liz Claiborne and Art Ortenenberg Foundation*
Most Stylish Dot.com Award *PleatsPlease.com*
Special Award The Dean of American Fashion *Bill Blass*
Special Award The American Regional Press presented to *Janet McCue*
Special Award *The Academy of Motion Picture Arts & Sciences* for Creating the World's Most Glamorous Fashion Show

1998/1999

Womenswear Designer of the Year *Michael Kors*
Menswear Designer of the Year *Calvin Klein*
Accessory Designer of the Year *Marc Jacobs*
Perry Ellis Award for Womenswear *Josh Patner and Bryan Bradley for Tuleh*
Perry Ellis Award for Menswear *Matt Nye*
Perry Ellis Award for Accessories *Tony Valentine*
International Designer of the Year *Yohji Yamamoto*
Lifetime Achievement Award *Yves Saint Laurent*
Eugenia Sheppard Award *Elsa Klensch*
Humanitarian Award *Liz Tilberis*
Special Award *Betsey Johnson* for her Timeless Talent
Special Award *Simon Doonan* for his Windows on Fashion
Special Award *InStyle Magazine* for Putting the Spotlight on Fashion and Hollywood
Special Award *Sophia Loren* for a Lifetime of Style
Special Award *Cher* for her Influence on Fashion

1997

Womenswear Designer of the Year *Marc Jacobs*
Menswear Designer of the Year *John Bartlett*
Accessory Designer of the Year *Kate Spade*
Perry Ellis Award for Womenswear *Narciso Rodriguez*
Perry Ellis Award for Menswear *Sandy Dalal*
International Designer of the Year *John Galliano*
Lifetime Achievement Award *Geoffrey Beene*
The Stiletto Award *Manolo Blahnik*
Special Award *Anna Wintour* for her Influence on Fashion
Dom Pérignon Award *Ralph Lauren*
Special Award *Elizabeth Taylor* for a Lifetime of Glamour
Special Tributes *Gianni Versace & Princess Diana*

1996

Womenswear Designer of the Year *Donna Karan*
Menswear Designer of the Year *Ralph Lauren*
Accessory Designer of the Year *Elsa Peretti for Tiffany & Co.*
Perry Ellis Award for Womenswear *Daryl Kerrigan for Daryl K.*
Perry Ellis Award for Menswear *Gene Meyer*
Perry Ellis Award for Accessories *Kari Sigerson and
Miranda Morrison for Sigerson Morrison*
International Designer of the Year *Helmut Lang*
Lifetime Achievement Award *Arnold Scaasi*
Eugenia Sheppard Award *Amy Spindler*
Dom Pérignon Award *Kenneth Cole*
Special Award *Richard Martin & Harold Koda*

1995

Womenswear Designer of the Year *Ralph Lauren*
Menswear Designer of the Year *Tommy Hilfiger*
Accessory Designer of the Year *Hush Puppies*
Perry Ellis Award for Womenswear *Marie-Anne Oudejans for Tocca*
Perry Ellis Award for Menswear *Richard Tyler /
Richard Bengtsson & Edward Pavlick for Richard Edwards (tie)*
Perry Ellis Award for Accessories *Kate Spade*
International Designer of the Year *Tom Ford for Gucci*
Lifetime Achievement Award *Hubert de Givenchy*
Eugenia Sheppard Award *Suzy Menkes*
Special Award *Isaac Mizrahi & Douglas Keeve for* Unzipped
Special Award *Robert Isabell*
Special Award *Lauren Bacall*
Dom Pérignon Award *Bill Blass*

1994

Womenswear Designer of the Year *Richard Tyler*
Perry Ellis Award for Womenswear *Victor Alfaro
and Cynthia Rowley (tie)*
Perry Ellis Award for Menswear *Robert Freda*
Accessory Award for Women *Robert Lee Morris*
Accessory Award for Men *Gene Meyer*
Lifetime Achievement Award
Carrie Donovan/Nonnie Moore/Bernadine Morris
Eugenia Sheppard Award *Patrick McCarthy*
Special Award *Elizabeth Tilberis*
Special Award *The Wonderbra*
Special Award *Kevyn Aucoin*
Special Tribute *Jacqueline Kennedy Onassis*

1993

Womenswear Designer of the Year *Calvin Klein*
Menswear Designer of the Year *Calvin Klein*
Perry Ellis Award for Womenswear *Richard Tyler*
Perry Ellis Award for Menswear *John Bartlett*
Lifetime Achievement Award
Judith Leiber/Polly Allen Mellen
International Award for Accessories *Prada*
Eugenia Sheppard Award *Bill Cunningham*
Special Awards *Fabien Baron/Adidas/Converse/Keds/Nike/Reebok*
Industry Tribute *Eleanor Lambert*

1992

Womenswear Designer of the Year *Marc Jacobs*
Menswear Designer of the Year *Donna Karan*
Accessory Designer of the Year *Chrome Hearts*
Perry Ellis Award *Anna Sui*
International Award *Gianni Versace*
Lifetime Achievement Award *Pauline Trigère*
Special Awards *Steven Meisel/Audrey Hepburn/
The Ribbon Project/Visual AIDS*

1991

Womenswear Designer of the Year *Isaac Mizrahi*
Menswear Designer of the Year *Roger Forsythe*
Accessory Designer of the Year *Karl Lagerfeld for House of Chanel*
Perry Ellis Award *Todd Oldham*
Lifetime Achievement Award *Ralph Lauren*
Eugenia Sheppard Award *Marylou Luther*
Special Awards *Marvin Traub/Harley Davidson/Jessye Norman/
Anjelica Huston/Judith Jamison*

1990

Womenswear Designer of the Year *Donna Karan*
Menswear Designer of the Year *Joseph Abboud*
Accessory Designer of the Year *Manolo Blahnik*
Perry Ellis Award *Christian Francis Roth*
Lifetime Achievement Award *Martha Graham*
Eugenia Sheppard Award *Genevieve Buck*
Special Awards *Emilio Pucci/Anna Wintour*
Special Tribute *Halston*

1989

Womenswear Designer of the Year *Isaac Mizrahi*
Menswear Designer of the Year *Joseph Abboud*
Accessory Designer of the Year *Paloma Picasso*
Perry Ellis Award *Gordon Henderson*
Lifetime Achievement Award *Oscar de la Renta*
Eugenia Sheppard Award *Carrie Donovan*
Special Award *The Gap*
Special Tribute *Giorgio di Sant'Angelo/Diana Vreeland*

1988

Menswear Designer of the Year *Bill Robinson*
Perry Ellis Award *Mizrahi*
Lifetime Achievement Award *Richard Avedon/Nancy Reagan*
Eugenia Sheppard Award *Nina Hyde*
Special Award *Geoffrey Beene/Karl Lagerfeld for House of Chanel/
Grace Mirabella/Judith Peabody/The Wool Bureau Inc.*

1987

Best American Collection *Calvin Klein*
Menswear Designer of the Year *Ronaldus Shamask*
Perry Ellis Award *Marc Jacobs*
Eugenia Sheppard Award *Bernadine Morris*
Lifetime Achievement Award *Giorgio Armani, Horst, Eleanor Lambert*
Special Awards *Arnell/Bickford Associates and Donna Karan/
Manolo Blahnik/Hebe Dorsey/FIT/Giorgio di Sant'Angelo/Arnold
Scaasi/Vanity Fair*
Special Tribute *Mrs. Vincent Astor*

1986

Perry Ellis Award *David Cameron (first recipient)*
Lifetime Achievement Award *Bill Blass/Marlene Dietrich*
Special Awards *Geoffrey Beene/Dalma Callado/Elle magazine/
Etta Froio/Donna Karan/Elsa Klensch/Christian Lacroix/
Ralph Lauren*

1985

Lifetime Achievement Award *Katharine Hepburn/
Alexander Liberman*
Special Tribute *Rudi Gernreich*
Special Awards *Geoffrey Beene/Liz Claiborne/Norma Kamali/Donna
Karan/Miami Vice/Robert Lee Morris/Ray-Ban Sunglasses/"Tango
Argentino"*

1984

Lifetime Achievement Award *James Galanos*
Special Tribute *Eugenia Sheppard*
Special Awards *Astor Place Hair Design/Bergdorf Goodman/Kitty
D'Alessio/John Fairchild/Annie Flanders/Peter Moore of NIKE/Robert
Pittman of MTV/Stephen Sprouse/Diana Vreeland/Bruce Weber*

1983

*Jeff Aquilon/Giorgio Armani/Diane De Witt/Perry Ellis/Calvin Klein/
Antonio Lopez/Issey Miyake/Patricia Underwood/Bruce Weber*

1982

*Bill Cunningham/Perry Ellis/Norma Kamali/Karl Lagerfeld/
Antonio Lopez*

1981

*Jhane Barnes/Perry Ellis/Andrew Fezza/Alexander Julian/Barry
Kieselstein-Cord/Calvin Klein/Nancy Knox/Ralph Lauren/Robert
Lighton/Alex Mate & Lee Brooks/Yves Saint Laurent/Fernando Sanchez*

CREDITS

Page 6: Roger Davies, courtesy of *Elle Decor*; page 8: Martyn Thompson; page 12-15: Courtesy Reem Acra; page 16-19: Photographs by Douglas Friedman; page 20-21: Oberto Gili/*House & Garden*; © Condé Nast; page 22-23: © Miki Duisterhof; page 24-25: Robert Wright; page 26-27: Don Freeman; page 28: Michael Simon (top), Andrew Fezza (bottom); page 29: Stefan Miljanic; page 30-33: Nigel Barker LLC; page 34-35: Roger Davies, courtesy of *Elle Decor*; page 36-37: Photographs by Douglas Friedman; page 38 (clockwise from top left): Ryan Lai, George Seferidis, and Miriam Ri, photo courtesy of Michael Crouser; page 39: Photo courtesy of Michael Crouser; page 40-41: Ryan Lai; page 42-45: Photographer: Sheila Metzner; page 46-49: Photos by Laura Resen; page 50: Jackie Rogers (top), Isaac Manevitz for Ben Amun (bottom); page 51: Alan K. Siegel; page 52-53: Francisco Valdez; page 54-55: Mikkel Vang/*Domino*; © Condé Nast; page 56: Photographs by Douglas Friedman; page 57: Martyn Thompson; page 58: Photographs by Douglas Friedman; page 59: Martyn Thompson; page 60-63: François Halard/Trish South Management www.TrunkArchive.com; page 64-65: Oberto Gili/*House & Garden*; © Condé Nast; page 66-69: Photos by Bärbel Miebach www.bärbelmiebach.com; page 70: William Waldron; page 71: Michael Spirito (top), Christian Kraust (bottom); page 72-73: Simon Upton/The Interior Archive; page 74-75: photo © Laurie Lambrecht, 2003; page 76-77: Esteban Solis, photographer, San Miguel de Allende, MX; page 78-79: Photo by Eric Piasecki; page 80-81: John Ellis www.johnellisphoto.com; page 82-83: Paul Costello, Suzuki K; page 84-87: Michel Arnaud; page 88: © Peter Aaron/Esto; page 89: Preston T. Phillips; page 90-93: François Halard/Trish South Management www.TrunkArchive.com; page 94-95: The Hutsons; page 96-97: Ngoc Minh Ngo; page 98-101: Photographed by Luca Pioltelli; page 102-105: Everett Fenton Gidley www.efg3.com; page 106: Howard Goldfarb/Ron Chereskin's Fire Island Pines summer home, 2005 (top), Sandra Müller (bottom); page 107: BowmanPhoto.com (top), Yigal Azrouël (bottom); page 108 (from top): © 2010 Chip Pankey Photography, Inc., PK Tigrett, Lord Derry Moore/*Architectural Digest*; © Condé Nast; page 109: © David Schilling courtesy of *Veranda*; page 110-111: Simon Upton/The Interior Archive; page 112-113: © 2001 PhilipHarvey.com; page 114-115: Photographs by Douglas Friedman; page 116-117: Pieter Estersohn; page 118-119: © Lucas Allen; page 120-125: Gilles de Chabaneix from the Ralph Lauren Archive; page 126: Henry Jacobson; page 127: Robin Renzi (top), Simon Chaput (bottom); page 128-131: William Waldron; 132-133: Pieter Estersohn; 134-135: Martyn Thompson; 136-137: © 2006 Mark Finkenstaedt www.mfpix.com; page 138-139: Melanie Acevedo; page 140: Sal and Nancy Cesarani (top), Karen Eisen (bottom); page 141: Anders Overgaard (top), Photo by Scott Sternberg (bottom); page 142-145: Melanie Acevedo; page 146-147: © Dick Busher 1989, Photograph: Albert Sanchez; page 148-149: Manuel Zublena/*Madame Figaro* (left), Photograph by Robert Astley Sparke (right); page 150: Photograph by Robert Astley Sparke; page 151: Manuel Zublena/*Madame Figaro*; page 152-155: Photo: Bjorg Magnea -www.bjorgmagnea.com; page 156-157: © Kim Sargent; page 158: William Waldron; page 159: Kyung Chung (top), Robert Rausch © 2009 (bottom); page 160-163: Mikkel Vang; page 164-165: Photographs by Gilles Bensimon; page 166-167: Michael Mundy; page 168-169: Roger Davies, courtesy of *Elle Decor*; page 170-171: Paul Morelli; page 172: Norman Jean Roy/www.trunkarchive.com; page 173-175: François Halard/Trish South Management www.TrunkArchive.com; page 176: Paul Nathan (top), John Whitledge (bottom); page 177: Robert Danes; page 178-181: Alexandre Bailhache/*House & Garden*; © Condé Nast; page 182-183: MRT Imaging; page 184-185: James Merrell; page 186-187: Paul Warchol; page 188-189: Laura Poretzky-Garcia; page 190-191: Pieter Estersohn; page 192-195: © 2010 Elizabeth Felicella Photography/Project Design: WORK Architecture Company; page 196-197: Roger Davies, courtesy of *Elle Decor*; page 198: Eric Domège (top), Dean Kaufman (bottom); page 199: William Waldron; page 200-201: Richie Gleason; page 202-205: Rick Guidotti; page 206-207: Photographs by Douglas Friedman; page 208-211: Photo by Annie Schlecter for *Metropolitan Home*. © Hachette Filipacchi Media U.S., Inc. Published with permission. All rights reserved.; page 212-213: Durston Saylor/*Architectural Digest*; © Condé Nast.; page 214-215: David Duncan Livingston; page 216: Photo by Katrin Zimmermann (top), Photo by Oleg March (bottom); page 217: http://www.jameswebstudio.com; page 218-219: Melanie Acevedo; page 220-221: Ted Yarwood – Photographer; page 222 (from top): Laura Moss (2), Mark Lund (1); page 223: Laura Moss; page 224-225: SHINO YANAGAWA (left), Roger Davies, courtesy of *Elle Decor* (right); page 226-227: Maria Snyder; page 228-231: © Noe DeWitt; page 232-233: Simon Upton/The Interior Archive; page 234: Belle Ombre (top), Libby Edelman (bottom); page 235: Scott Frances/*Architectural Digest*; © Condé Nast; page 236-237: Melanie Acevedo; page 238-241: Matthew Williams; page 242-245: Gordon Thompson III; page 246-247: Tim Street-Porter; page 248-249: Roger Davies, courtesy of *Elle Decor*; page 250-251: William Waldron; page 252: George Sharp (top), Mimi So Home (bottom); page 253: Keanan Duffty; page 254-257: Timothy Kolk; page 258-263: François Halard/Trish South Management www.TrunkArchive.com; page 264-267: © Paul Warchol; page 268: Joel Barhamand (top), Photograph by Jon Heil (bottom); page 269: Kevin Sinclair.

ACKNOWLEDGMENTS

I am honored to invite you into the homes of our members with the publication of *American Fashion: Designers at Home*. I am grateful to the designers for opening their doors and letting us see where they live and that their creativity extends beyond clothing and accessories. This is the sixth book that the Council of Fashion Designers of America has published with Assouline and it is the latest in the very popular American Fashion series. Our other books are *American Fashion, American Fashion Accessories, American Fashion Menswear, American Fashion Cookbook* and *Geoffrey Beene: An American Fashion Rebel*. CFDA is blessed to work under the guidance of Prosper and Martine Assouline and our editor Esther Kremer. They have been great partners on all our books. Thanks also to Naomi Leibowitz and Camille Dubois at Assouline for their work on this book.

So many of the photos in the book have come from *Elle Decor* and we are so appreciative that the magazine has agreed to share their work with us. Thanks to the many other magazines which also allowed us access to their work, including *Architectural Digest, House & Garden, InStyle, Metropolitan Home, Town & Country* and *Vogue*. None of our books would be possible without the support of the photographers who continue to be generous in allowing us to use their work. We are forever appreciative for their kindness and talent.

At the CFDA we work under the leadership of our president, Diane von Furstenberg. Having had the good fortune to spend time at her Connecticut home, which is featured in this book, I can say firsthand that she is as warm and welcoming in person as you can imagine from the beautiful environment she has created for herself. Diane inspires the CFDA staff everyday and I thank her for her leadership. The CFDA staff works tirelessly on behalf of the organization. Thank you to Lisa Smilor, CaSandra Diggs, Catherine Bennett, Amy Ondocin, Danielle Billinkoff, Sarah Maniatty, Johanna Stout, Nancy Caton, and Heather Jacobson for your loyalty and professionalism. An extra big thanks to CFDA staff Karen Peterson for bringing her home experience to the CFDA, Christine Olsen for the day-to-day management of putting this book together, and to Sarah Yoon for her organization and help. If it were not for Christine and Sarah, there would be no book for you to see right now.

With each of our books we have been lucky to work with the best writers in their field, and *American Fashion: Designers at Home* is no exception. Rima Suqi spent countless hours talking to the designers to share with you their personal glimpses and stories. We respect her unique and stylish point of view, which is more than evident in this book. Thank you, Rima.

My biggest thank you goes to Margaret Russell, the editor in chief of *Elle Decor*. I have known Margaret for almost twenty years at various stages in my career and can say she is one of the nicest and most giving people I have ever worked with. Her sense of sophistication and passion for design has been a major influence in how the world looks at interiors, decoration, architecture, and product design. We could think of no one more qualified to write the foreword for this book than Margaret and this book would not be possible without her cooperation.

STEVEN KOLB
Executive Director

A huge thank you first and foremost to Steven Kolb and Karen Peterson at the CFDA for thinking of me to write this book. There are many others you could have asked, and I'm selfishly glad (or blissfully ignorant) that you didn't. Christine Olsen, also at the CFDA, who worked seemingly tirelessly to organize (and reorganize) designers and images and contacts—this book would not exist without you.

To the Assouline team: Esther Kremer for editorial guidance, Naomi Leibowitz for staying on top of all those photos, and Camille Dubois for gorgeous layouts.

To Valerie Steele and Helen Lane at FIT, both for research direction and access to the library. To Paul Rothenberg for his wisely chosen words and sage advice. And finally to all the designers featured within for access, information, and page after page of inspirational rooms.

RIMA SUQI